Yugoslavia: Dalmatian Coast

From Zadar to the Makarska Riviera
including the Dalmatian Islands

D1352982

Jarrold Publishing

CONTENTS

Hvar

This is Dalmatia

As you look out of the aircraft, a grey, rugged range of mountains meets your gaze. In between the mountains can be seen the clefts of valleys bespeckled with patches of green, bereft of houses, rather like a lunar landscape. Suddenly you see the coast road, a small town, islands. A ship passes through on the sea below, leaving a trail of foam in its wake. Reefs, more isles — and then the mainland reappears. A few minutes later the jet comes down to land on the runway of Zadar airport.

During this approach to the mainland over the coastal mountains and turning over the sea, visitors have this photogenic glimpse of the countryside of Dalmatia, which forms part of the Yugoslavian republic of Croatia. Those hungry for sun on the rocky beaches of this region can see numerous islands.

Looking inland from many places along the coast, you can see the ridges and peaks of the karst mountains, often rising to a height of 1000 metres and even higher. Many holidaymakers are unaware that wide, fertile valleys run parallel to the coast, often as little as 30 kilometres inland. These depressions are known as *polje*, in which water, running down through natural underground channels, collects on the porous rock formations.

At first glance the offshore islands present the coastal visitor with only half of their

Golden Horn Beach, Bol

scenic character. From the mainland they appear grey and chilly, as their inland green areas are invisible. In these stark contrasts between desolate rock and fertile retreats live the Dalmatians, an open and spirited race of people, whose past has been moulded by Illyrian, Slavonic, Roman and, above all, Venetian influences. This impressive countryside is the Mecca of many sun-seeking holidaymakers, who stream year after year into the numerous seaside hotels and fill the promenades.

Bathing in the sea is fun here. Apart from the town areas of Trogir, Šibenik and Split the water is crystal-clear and clean, for Yugoslavia has become environment-conscious. Today no hotel pipes untreated waste into the Adriatic.

Only very few multi-storeyed tower blocks, with their unimaginative flat roofs, a legacy of the early sixties, rise out of their surroundings. Most of the more recent houses have the typical red-tiled roofs. Unfortunately, in recent years many once-romantic harbours along the Dalmatian coast have become marinas which provide shelter for giant armadas of yachts and small motor-boats during the holiday season. The former fishing villages, about which many holiday brochures still enthuse, are long since gone. Although you can see everywhere the more recent attempts by the authorities to preserve the historic buildings, it is, nevertheless, all too obvious that the beautiful land of Dalmatia is today dedicated to serving the tourist.

Essential details in brief

Name:
Dalmatia is the name given to the Mediterranean region within the Socialist Republic of Croatia, one of the six constituent republics forming the Federal Republic of Yugoslavia.

Type of State:
A Socialist federal state, orientated in its foreign policy towards the group of non-aligned countries.

Government:
Collective state government with diminishing influence of the Communists, the only permitted party up to 1989. Decentralisation of government since 1963, with a growing tendency towards economic self-determination on the part of the constituent republics. The highest offices in government, administration and party are shared amongst the national and constituent republics in accordance with the rotation principle.

Language:
Croat and Serbo-Croat in Croatia, also Italian on the coast. Serbo-Croat is one of the three official languages of Yugoslavia (the others are Slovene and Macedonian).

Religion:
The Christians in Croatia belong almost exclusively to the Roman Catholic Church.

Population:
Croatia 4.6 million (Yugoslavia 23.12 million).

Capital:
Croatia: Zagreb (Yugoslavia: Belgrade).

Area:
Croatia: 56,538 sq. km (22% of total area of Yugoslavia which is 255,804 sq. km; U.K. 242,496 sq. km).

Economy:
The industry of Croatia is concentrated in the Pannonic Basin, with Zagreb as the centre, and in the coastal towns. Agriculture dominates in the plains and in the central mountains, and the tourist economy on the Adriatic.

Inflation:
The rate of inflation has climbed from 21.9% (1980) to 250% (beginning of 1989). As a result of the favourable exchange rates, which alter almost daily, tourists are largely untouched by the effects of this.

6

Although Dalmatia, which owes its name to the Illyrian tribe of the Delmats or Dalmats, is not a federated state of the Federal Republic of Yugoslavia in its own right, but belongs to Croatia, it nevertheless has its own character and its own history, moulded by an uninterrupted occupation by various foreigners.

About 1200 B.C.: Illyrian tribes (Indo-Germanic) occupy the West Balkans.

4th c. B.C: Greek colonists found trading-posts (*Pharos*/Hvar, *Idassa*/Zadar, *Tragurion*/Trogir, *Salonae*/Solin).

3rd c. B.C.–5th c. A.D: After the intervention of Rome in Illyrian-Greek conflicts, Roman colonisation of the coast begins. In the 1st c. B.C. 'Illyricum' becomes a Roman province which later provides six Roman emperors, including Diocletian (A.D. 284–305, palace in Split). After the end of the western Empire in 476, Byzantium gains increasing influence.

6th–7th c: From 537 under Byzantine administration. South Slavonic tribes (Yugo-Slavs) set foot in the Yugoslavia of today.

8th–9th c: Temporarily under the rule of the Carolingians, against whom the Croatian tribes unite under Prince Posavski. At the end of the 9th c. Pannonia and Dalmatia amalgamate under Prince Tomislav.

10th–11th c: 925 Tomislav becomes the first king of Croatia. About 1000 the first attacks by the Venetians on the Dalmatian ports. Internal unrest in Croatia leads to an alliance with the kingdom of Hungary.

12th–13th c: 1102 the coronation of King Koloman of Hungary-Croatia. 1202 the 4th Crusade under the Doge of Venice, Enrico Dandolo, the destruction of Zadar, further attacks on the coastal towns. 1204 the Crusaders conquer Constantinople. 1205 the capture of Dubrovnik, which has a Venetian governor until 1358.

14th–18th c: 1353 to 1391 the Bosnian Ban Tvrtko rules on the coast from Kotor to Split. The Turks push inland. From 1420 Venice rules the whole Dalmatian coast with the sole exception of Dubrovnik, which is able to retain its independence. Croat-Dalmatian defensive actions against Turkish attacks last until the 18th c. 1797 Dalmatia and Venice fall to Austria.

19th and 20th c: 1809 Dalmatia is incorporated into the 'Illyrian Province' of Napoleon. After the Congress of Vienna 1814/15 Dalmatia returns to Austria and becomes a Crown Land of the Hapsburgs. Attempts at national unification end in 1918 with the Proclamation of the Kingdom of Yugoslavia (Serbia, Croatia and Slovenia). 1941 occupation of Yugoslavia by German and Italian troops, struggle for liberation by the Communist partisan army. 1945 foundation of the Federal Republic of Yugoslavia, composed of the six People's Republics of Slovenia, Croatia, Serbia, Bosnia/Hercegovina, Montenegro and Macedonia.

Holidays in Dalmatia

It was no accident that more than a hundred years ago the Adriatic coast of Yugoslavia was found to be a very pleasant place in which to spend the winter, for in spite of its comparatively northern situation it enjoys an extraordinarily favourable climate as the result of a warm ocean current. Protected by the bleak mountains which keep the wind at bay, a rich subtropical flora has blossomed. The Adriatic stores the heat of the summer and releases it in winter, so that even in January the temperature very seldom drops to freezing point. In summer the effect is reversed, the sea acting as a coolant. The area has an annual average of more than 2000 hours of sunshine.

The holiday season on the Yugoslavian Adriatic coast is from April to October. In the height of summer the seaside resorts and camping sites are filled to overflowing. Winter sports are possible in the mountainous regions from December to March.

Between the fjord of Starigrad-Paklenica, north of Zadar, and the Kotor coastal gap lies a stretch of countryside which is suitable for holidays all the year round. Some 100 hotels in Dalmatia will take guests in winter. Mainly local people, but nowadays an increasing number of foreigners as well, take their holidays here during the cold part

Enjoying a picnic on Brač

of the year. More and more health-resort visitors take advantage of the lower prices at that time of year — on Hvar or in Igalo on the Bay of Kotor — and relax in one of the hotels, most of which are equipped with indoor pools and areas for sport.

As more private board and lodging has been provided, the amount of accommodation available on the coast has increased dramatically in the past few years. Anyone who wishes to holiday here in the high season must be prepared for the onslaught of mass tourism. Temporary annoyances should perhaps then be accepted as being mere trifles — with a *'nema problema'* (no problem) as the Yugoslavs say. Watch how the locals deal with problems: there is a way around everything.

From April to June, when the yellow broom is in blossom, it is warm and truly restful in Dalmatia. This is when those who really know the area come, even though the sea is not yet ideal for swimming. September and October are also good months for a holiday. That is when the hotel staff again have time to provide an individual service, and the families running guesthouses can sit down and have a chat with their guests. The hectic rush of the high season is over; the days are shorter, but it is still warm. Swimming in the sea can be pleasant up to early November. Campers may have difficulty in finding sites still open after the middle of October. The leisure park of Dubrovnik is open all the year round.

Holidays with children

The Dalmatian coast, most of which is steeply sloping and rocky, is not ideal for small children who cannot swim. At some places on the Makarska Riviera sand is spread between the rocks all the year round, in order to make the beaches more 'user friendly', but even this is unsuitable for youngsters, if not dangerous, for at the end of the sand there is usually a steep fall into deep water.

Practically all hotels on the coast are prepared to negotiate with parents over price. Even when they describe themselves as 'catering for children', this does not necessarily mean that the accommodation is adequate for children's special needs.

The Club Méditerranée lists suitable holidays for children in its brochures; the straw-hut villages of Pakoštane (north of Split) and Sveti Marko (on the island of Tivat) take children aged from four to ten in their Mini-Clubs and from ten to twelve in the Kids' Clubs. In Pakoštane children between two and four are also catered for.

How the people live

To visitors from the United Kingdom, and people from many other countries who spend their summer holidays there, the whole Adriatic coast of Yugoslavia, from Umag in the north to Ulcinj in the south, looks like the edge of a giant pool that is fully equipped for bathing, surfing and sailing; a picturesque setting for a carefree holiday under the southern sun. As in many other areas of the world, at certain times of the year the number of holidaymakers is many times greater than that of the local population.

Relatively few visitors realise that in the place where they are staying, which was praised in their holiday brochure as being an 'old fishing town', there are no real fishing boats; neither do they realise that the man at the bar, when asked which local restaurant he recommends, just shrugs his shoulders because he hails from a completely different part of Yugoslavia and works on the coast for only three months in the year. A journey from north to south in mid-October, when the sun still shines

Traditional local character — girls in national dress, haymaking, tomatoes by boat, and peppers in the market

strongly over the Adriatic coast, leads you to realise, when you see the relatively empty streets and bars, that the coast is actually quite thinly populated. With the exception of the larger towns, the sun-balcony of Yugoslavia today really only offers work in tourism, and then only for a few summer months each year, even though more and more of the larger hotels, equipped with indoor swimming pools, conference rooms and sports halls, are staying open all the year round.

Holidaymakers in Yugoslavia today seldom have any idea what the coast looked like in the recent past. For example, few people know that the last section of the Adria-Magistrale (Adriatic Coastal Highway) connecting Bar and Ulcinj was not completed until 1976.

The infrastructure

Previously, anyone wishing to get to Ulcinj, the most southerly holiday resort in Yugoslavia with the only long and sandy beach in the whole country, had to struggle along an indifferent road through the hinterland.

Ever since the forests were cut down at the time of the first Greek settlements, the islands off the coast have been sparsely populated. There was a lack of fertile springs and only as many people lived on the islands as could be provided with water from the wells. Today many islands obtain piped water from the mainland and in summer the visitors outnumber the local people by ten to one.

Even in the last century, travelling to places on the coast nearly always meant going by sea. Although the coastal resorts all had roads connecting them with the interior, they were not linked to each other. Until the end of the Second World War tourism was confined to a few places in Istria, such as Opatija and Portorož. Not until the construction of the coast-road, which was started in the north in 1951 and gradually pushed south, did the countless hotels go up, some made of unsuitable building materials. Tourism left untouched the traditional character of the old town centres and, in part, the old harbour districts, but just behind them indiscriminate building took place, without proper thought for the future. However, in the late sixties and early seventies, reports in the Yugoslavian press of the way the coast of Spain was being ruined led to a sense of environmental awareness on the part of the authorities and the people.

Many a poorly designed building bears witness to the uncontrolled boom in the early years of tourism on the coast. Since then private enterprise has made itself felt everywhere on the Adriatic; in the increase in the number of private apartments and the provision of small camping-sites, as well the establishment of guest-houses, restaurants and shops of all kinds.

Changes in the economy

A fundamental constitutional amendment passed by the Yugoslavian parliament on November 25th 1988 aims at replacing the former state-planned economy with a market economy, and the encouragement of private investment.

Previously, businesses in the craft sector, industry, the catering trade and tourism were allowed to employ up to ten people who were not members of the family. That number is now twenty and so it has even become possible to run small hotels. But inflation has meant that all good things come to an end and it is now impossible to obtain loans at reasonable rates of interest, and only someone who has earned western currency abroad is in a position to build privately.

Until 1988 the workers' councils had a decisive influence, as they did throughout the Yugoslavian economy, in the larger hotel complexes on the coast, which often also run cafés, supermarkets, restaurants, camping-sites and boat-hire stations. Among other things, the councils decided each year how the profits should be used, as a result of which the money was frequently divided among the work-force instead of being reserved for urgently needed new investment. Since the amendment in the constitution, the degree of management control has been strengthened, even though the workers' administration still has the last word.

Now it is even possible for there to be foreign shareholdings in excess of the 49% blocking minority. Hope rests on foreign capital, with investors now able to fill the important posts in the business with people in whom they have confidence, and they can transfer profits abroad.

In agriculture, farmers may now cultivate up to thirty hectares of their own land. This item in the constitutional amendment is of little importance for the coast, because here most of the vineyards and small areas devoted to fruit-growing have always been privately run.

Ethnic problems

In Yugoslavia today, much is in a state of flux. On December 31st 1988, for the first time since the war, the whole Yugoslavian government resigned. This was preceded by resignations of party leadership committees and civil servants in all the constituent republics. The country's economic crisis has been followed by a political crisis, the cause of which can be traced largely to economic rivalries between the country's various nationalities.

Since the founding of the Federal People's Republic of Yugoslavia under the then Prime Minister and later Head of State Marshal Tito, on November 25th 1945, members of the different nationalities, languages and religions have been united under the federal state then created. According to the last census in 1981, the following picture emerged in the six republics and in the autonomous provinces of Vojvodina and Kosovo:

Slovenia: Pop. 1.9 million; Slovenes 90.5%, Croats 2.9%, Serbs 2.2%, others 4.4%.
Croatia: Pop. 4.6 million; Croats 75%, Serbs 11.5%, others 13.5%.
Bosnia-Hercegovina: Pop. 4.1 million; Muslims 39.5% (the Muslims have been recognised as an ethnic group since 1981), Serbs 32.2%, Croats 18.3%, others 10%.
Serbia: Pop. 5.7 million; Serbs 66.4%, Albanians 14%, Hungarians 4%, others 15.6%.
Montenegro: Pop. 600,000; Montenegrins 68.5%, Muslims 13.4% (see above), Albanians 6.5%, Serbs 3.3%, others 8.3%.
Macedonia: Pop. 2 million; Macedonians 67.2%, Albanians 19.8%, Turks 4.5%, Serbs 2.3%, others 6.2%.
Autonomous Province of Vojvodina: Pop. 2 million; Serbs 54.1%, Hungarians 18.9%, Croats 5.4%, Slovacs 3.4%, Romanians 2.3%, others 15.9%.
Autonomous Province of Kosovo: Pop. 1.6 million; Albanians 77.5%, Serbs 13.2%, Muslims 7% (see above), Montenegrins 1.7%, others (mainly Turks) 3.9%.

On the coast during the busy season the foreign visitor will meet very few Yugoslav holidaymakers, except in a few places such as Neum where many officials have built villas. The reason is simple: hotel prices are just too high for the majority. However, outside the summer season and even in the winter Yugoslavs fill many of those hotels which stay open all the year. Then, visitors who speak German can meet people from all parts of this multi-national state for the older people often understand that language. Many of the younger people who spend time in the hotels while training for sport speak good English.

In the past it was often said that the people of the Dalmatian coast lacked hospitality and openness, and that they were easy-going and work-shy. This cliché is no longer true, if indeed it ever was. In the legions of workers serving the holidaymaker on the coast there are very few who actually hail from Dalmatia, and the young people are leaving for places where they are not threatened by nine months' unemployment just because the visitors have gone.

🦜 Phases of Art and Culture

For most holidaymakers in Dalmatia, the main reason for their trip is probably not the art treasures of the region, but nevertheless there is quite a range of relics from the past which are well worth seeing, even if it means sacrificing a few days on the beach.

Pre- and Early History

Unfortunately, not much remains from the Illyrian and Greek occupation other than overgrown burial-mounds, remains of walls and a few museum pieces such as the Kairos relief in Trogir.

The Roman period

Zadar was one of the first Roman bases on the Dalmatian coast. Even today the right-angled network of roads in the Old Town still follows the Roman layout, and the forum is still recognisable. However, Zadar cannot compete with Split, for the very heart of Dalmatia's capital is the palace of the Emperor Diocletian. Diocletian (A.D. 284-305), the last soldier-emperor, reformer and reorganiser of the Roman Empire, was a fascinating figure, having been described as 'possessing the varied characteristics of an Asiatic gourmand, a farm labourer, an enlightened despot, an artist and a sage'. Diocletian had the palace erected in the latter years of his reign, so that he could retire there after his abdication.

The huge complex, extended and converted over the centuries into a town of more than 3000 citizens, was both a luxurious castle and a fortress. It is one of the most important and splendid examples of late-Roman architecture. A strong surrounding wall with four double gates (each flanked by two octagonal watchtowers), four corner bastions and twelve towers protected this irregular rectangle of vast proportions (38,000 sq.m). The southern half was reserved for the emperor. Here were his living quarters and the places of worship; east of the peristyle was the mausoleum, which he had built in his lifetime, and to the west the Temple of Jupiter and two round temples (no longer in existence) dedicated to the goddesses Venus and Cybele. In the northern half were the buildings housing the military personnel and the servants.

The inner courtyard (peristyle), the mausoleum (cathedral), the Temple of Jupiter (baptistry), the remains of the walls and the mighty supports of the south front still give us a clear impression of its former glory.

The Early Christian period

Here we must mention Solin *(Salonae)*, the most important archaeological zone in Dalmatia, once the capital of the Roman province of *Illyricum*, then the centre of early Christendom in Dalmatia and a diocesan town. Burial grounds, in particular, have been found here, the most important being the sepulchral basilicas of Marusinac and Manastirine, as well as a complex of sacred buildings. Leaving Split, the well-signposted archaeological site lying at the end of the main road from the Zadar direction can also be reached by service bus. The most important finds, however, are housed in the Archaeological Museum in Split.

The Carolingian period

Perhaps one of the most curious buildings in all Europe is the castle-like 9th c. church of Sv. (*sveti* = saint) Donat in Zadar, a round building with three apses reaching up to

Diocletian's Palace, Split

the top storey, built by Donatus, then bishop of the city. The austere cylindrical interior with its ambulatory and gallery is reminiscent of the chapel in the palace of Charlemagne in Aachen. It is clear that Bishop Donatus got his idea for the building from this source, for he was the negotiator between Charlemagne and Byzantium, which regained Zadar under the Treaty of Aachen in 812.

Romanesque

Dalmatia can offer a whole series of outstanding examples of Romanesque — especially late Romanesque — art. This period was the heyday of Dalmatian art. As well as many precious woodcarvings, the most beautiful of which is the door of the cathedral of Andrija Buvina (1214), there are important architectural works including the cathedral of Sv. Stošija of Sadar (13th/14th c.) and Trogir Cathedral (started in 1123) with its marvellous portal designed by the master craftsman Radovan (1240).

Gothic and Renaissance

While these epochs of style on the coast show considerable Venetian influence, there is nevertheless a strong Croatian variation which comes from the master-builders and sculptors Juraj Dalmatinac (died 1473), Nikola Firentinac (died 1505) and

Andrija Aleši (ca. 1430–1504). The many examples include the cathedral at Šibenik, the patrician palaces of Trogir and Split, the Sponza and the Rector's Palace in Dubrovnik. It is interesting to observe how the long-established building tradition, which for a long time could not free itself from the Romanesque, changed to Gothic under Venetian influence. The decoration becomes richer, but the principle remains the same: delicate bow-windows, balconies and galleries providing relief for the wall surfaces.

Baroque

The Baroque period was the time of the Turkish Wars. Nevertheless, this period provided some buildings of note, such as the Cathedral of Our Lady and the Church of Saint Blaise, the town-patron, in Dubrovnik, as well as the palaces of the patrician families Cindro and Milesi in Split.

The Church of Saint Blaise, Dubrovnik

🍴 Food and Drink

Hors d'oeuvres, desserts, entrées

Čorbas: tangy soups, especially *Riblja čorba*, a fish soup.
Pršut: Dalmatian smoked ham.
Paški Sir: a goat's milk cheese from the island of Pag.
Pita: various kinds of puff-pastry, e.g. *Baklava* (with honey and nuts).
Musaka: a baked vegetable dish with aubergines, rice, minced meat and a sauce of sour cream.

Main courses

Čevapčići (shevapshishi): barbecued rolls of various kinds of minced meat, richly spiced, with raw, finely chopped onions.
Čulbastija (shulbasteeya): grilled pork, beef or veal steak with raw onions.
Djuveč (dshoovesh): vegetable stew with various meats and peppers.
Hajduški čevap (heydooshkyshevap): various kinds of barbecued meat.
Kapama: browned or boiled pieces of lamb, simmered with onions, spinach and vinegar, and served with sour cream or Kajmak.
Mučkalica (mooshkalitza): the flesh of onions strongly spiced with chillies and pepper (thus the name 'Tortured Spirit').
Pilav: rice stir-fried and then boiled with meat.
Plavi patlidžani punjeni (patlidsharny): stuffed aubergines.
Pljeskavica (plyeskavitza): minced pork and veal is shaped into flat balls, grilled both sides on the barbecue and served with finely chopped onions.
Ražnjići (rashnyitshee): spit-roasted pieces of pork, beef and veal, with raw onions.
Sarma: minced meat, heavily spiced and simmered in wine and cabbage leaves, and covered in a sauce of sour cream.
Sataraž (sattarash): onions simmered in oil, sliced paprika and tomatoes, with whisked eggs or slices of sausage.

Drinks

Dalmatian wines: Dingač, Kabernet, Plavac and *Babič* (primošten, red); *Grk* (island of Hvar), *Vugave* (white); *Prošek* (dessert wine).
Spirits: Maraškin, the famous liqueur made from maraschino cherries; *Šljivovica* (Slivovitz), double-distilled plum brandy, almost a national drink.

Fresh fruit and vegetables for sale

Fish of the Adriatic

It has been known for some time that the fish's 'labyrinth', the organ controlling its senses of gravity and rotation, acts as its hearing. Moreover, many fish are by no means dumb, but give out sounds to warn, scare off or attract one another. One of these, the umber fish, produces sounds with the aid of an unusually constructed air-bladder — sounds which play a role in reproduction: males and females find each other 'musically', so to speak.

The umber, or eagle-ray, is only one of some 365 species of denizens of the deep which inhabit the Yugoslavian Adriatic coast, so rich in fish — 120 of them are edible.

The various kinds of fish are prepared in many ways. The following can be can be enjoyed as *bouillabaisse* or *brodet*, as it is called in Croatian, with maize-porridge as a side-dish: umber, large sar-bream, brown perch and wrasse, grey mullet and moray or sea-eel.

Boiled: wolf perch, golden bream and umber.

Roasted: a special delicacy is the biting moray, prized by the Romans, but feared by fishermen and divers.

On the spit: gold-flecked grey mullet, sar and other bream.

Fried: mackerel in particular.

The taste-buds will also be tickled by the oysters and various species of mussel, and by snails, crabs, crayfish, lobsters, prawns and squid.

Thanks to a rigorous ban on fishing for a number of years, the fish stocks, which were decimated after the Second World War, have now recovered sufficiently to enable the small Yugoslavian fishing fleets once more to enrich the menus of coastal hotels and the markets of some of the towns inland.

Divers will find conditions ideal off the Kornati islands where they will be able to observe some thirty species:

Fish swimming near the surface: grey mullet, pearl fish or pike, tuna, swordfish, wolf and other perch.

Fish swimming at average depths: golden bream, forked mackerel and seriola.

Fish living among the rocks: dragon-head, brown jagged-perch, umber, large and small bream, moray and eel.

Fish living among the seaweed: brown and green wrasse, bream, sea or red barbel, of which Seneca said: 'There is nothing more beautiful than a dying barbel! As it struggles against approaching death, its exertions produce a shining crimson

Fish on the barbecue griddle

through its body, which later changes to a general pallor, with the most magnificent shades spreading as it dies'.

Fish living in the sand: rays, sea-dragons and dogfish.

Some thirty species of shark live in the Adriatic. However, because of the noise from the many boats, those which are dangerous to humans stay away from the coast. Unfortunately, the din has also driven the dolphins away, and they are seldom seen accompanying an excursion ship.

Mediterranean flora

The Dalmatian coast and the offshore islands consist solely of karst (porous rock with underground drainage and many cavities). When in the 4th c. B.C. the Greeks established the first trading posts here, many of the islands and also the western mountain slopes were wooded, in spite of the porous chalk. However, the trees were destroyed as a result of ship-building, and the thin layer of humus on top of the rock was washed away by rain. Not until the 1970s was a systematic reafforestation programme introduced, and this suffered severe setbacks because of forest fires along the coast, especially on the Makarska Riviera.

The oleander, cypress and olive trees, laurel and holm oaks, as well as the shrubs of the macchia and garigue, have belonged since ancient times to the native Mediterranean flora. Macchia and garigue evergreen, mainly rough undergrowth, cover wide areas of the Dalmatian coast and islands. Kermes oaks, strawberry plants, tree heathers, carob trees, pistachios, species of myrtle, broom and juniper grow here; also scented herbs, such as pale purple sage, aromatic thyme, rosemary growing to a height of almost two metres, and lavender bushes which when seen from a distance resemble velvety cushions of a silvery-blue.

The pomegranate tree, the name of which perhaps does not do justice to the pleasant taste of its fruit — the best-known pomegranate is no doubt that which the Trojan prince *Paris* gave to the goddess *Aphrodite* as the prize for her beauty — has also been native to the eastern Mediterranean since time immemorial. From the time of the ancient Egyptians up to that of the Gothic western world it was held in high symbolic esteem, as a sign of fertility, life and eternity, thanks to its extraordinary abundance. The pomegranate pattern on expensive textiles was equally popular with orientals and Christians for centuries.

Most of the other plants which are characteristic of the landscape found on the Mediterranean coast are strangers imported from far-off lands over the centuries.

The agave first reached Europe after the conquest of Mexico in the 16th c. It takes ten or twelve years before a tall candelabrum of blooms issues forth from the dagger-like crest of leaves; the agave blooms but once, and then dies.

The fig-cactus (opuntia) is the only species of cactus which grows wild by the Mediterranean.

The various types of palm trees growing along the broad promenades come from Africa, Australia, south-east Asia and California.

For its viticulture Dalmatia can probably thank the Greek colonists, who laid down the first vineyards on Viš.

Almond trees, resplendent as early as February with their array of pinkish-white flowers, citrus fruits, apples, pears, cherries (the famous maraschino liqueur comes from the maraska cherry), figs, apricots, peaches and, of

Lavender

Sword dance at a summer festival

course, plums (the basis of Šljivovica brandy) all ripen in the few fertile regions of Dalmatia. Lavender is cultivated on the island of Hvar.

There are 6000 known varieties of coastal vegetation. Armed with this information, you can sit peacefully in the shade of the Aleppo pines and tamarisks which line the beaches and, to the accompaniment of the warbling of the cicadas, try to have your midday nap.

Festivals and Folklore

The best known is the *summer festival* at Split, with international theatrical and concert performances in the striking setting of the colonnaded courtyard (peristyle) of the Palace of Diocletian. There are also other open-air stages. An *International Festival of Light Music* is held in Split in the first half of August.

The *Alka festival*, held in Sinj every year on the Sunday nearest to August 15th, commemorates a great victory over the Turks, and includes jousting by knights in old costumes and using old weapons (see Split).

For some years now Omiš has organised a big *folk music and dancing competition* in the second half of July, in which the best groups in Dalmatia take part.

Health cures

The biggest and best-known health centre for multi-disciplinary treatment in Yugoslavia is 50 km south of Dubrovnik, on Kotor Fjord in Igalo near Herzegnovi. Here the treatments advertised are mainly for motorial illnesses, breathing, heart and vascular problems, gynaecological disorders and minor skin complaints. Even beauty programmes and slimming cures are offered.

On the island of Hvar there is an allergological institute for treating diseases of the respiratory tract. Many patients prefer Hvar in winter because snow hardly ever falls there and the thermometer drops below zero only every few years. If, contrary to expectations, this does happen, the guest has the cost of accommodation refunded. So far, however, the hoteliers have not had to pay out very often. In all the larger towns in Dalmatia there is always one hotel which stays open through the winter.

Evening entertainment

You should not fail to see and hear the various music groups which perform during the high season on the terraces of seaside hotels. Because this sometimes rather noisy pleasure is not for those who like to go to bed early, with only a few exceptions the music finishes at 11 p.m., and the authorities have banished most discos to soundproof basements.

More and more places are now offering their guests more sophisticated entertainment. You can watch Dalmatian folk groups, or join in a group excursion from the coast to a traditional bar inland, where you can have plenty to eat and drink in a very lively atmosphere.

You can also visit the cinema in Yugoslavia without understanding the language, because in many places films are shown with the original dialogue and sub-titles in English. The same applies to T.V. films.

Shopping and Souvenirs

The colourful, traditional handmade articles make particularly pretty souvenirs. The silver filigree jewellery with coral and amber inlay is both beautiful and original. Other souvenirs worth recommending are copperware (e.g. a little pot for Turkish coffee), wooden articles, ceramics, basketwork, leather goods, handwoven colourful carpets and lace of all shapes and sizes.

You should attempt to trade and haggle only with itinerant dealers and sales-stands. Of course, in Yugoslavia as in other countries, most goods offered for sale as handmade are produced industrially. However, you can be sure that woollen goods and embroidery which the country women bring to market are genuine.

Sporting activities

Apart from underwater fishing, which is prohibited, and water-skiing, which has become somewhat unfashionable, all kinds of water-sports are available on the Dalmatian coast. At many places you can hire everything from a surfboard to a motor yacht with cabins in which to sleep. Sports equipment manufactured in Yugoslavia, and on offer in the holiday resorts, has for a long time been able to compete in quality with western products.

Most larger hotels have tennis courts, although not all are yet floodlit for playing in the cooler hours of the evening. Volleyball pitches are also often available; this sport is much more popular in Yugoslavia than in Britain. Teams are frequently made up of locals and holidaymakers. There are some 100 firms along the coast offering water-sport facilities. More details about schools for sailing and windsurfing and

Souvenirs are found everywhere

Sailing from Vrboska

chartering possibilities can be obtained from (among others): ACY-Marina YU-58000 Split.

There are only a few places where bicycles can be hired. There are fewer riding-stables on the coast than inland; one can be found in the little town of Sinj, 32 km east of Split.

For those who like hill-climbing, rather than lying in the sun all day, there is a tour into the karst area inland from the coast; coming from the north along the Adria-Magistrale, in Karlobag you take the road to the left to Gospić. You drive round numerous bends, with magnificent views over the sea, up into the mountain pass (1000 m). Suddenly, the stony desert beyond changes into an idyllic green oasis; in the midst of meadows and lightly wooded uplands lies the mountain hotel of Velebno in Baške Oštarije, a centre for hill-walkers, who can set out from here to explore the countryside along numerous, well-marked trails.

You can also go by car from Starigrad to the car-park at the entrance to Paklenica National Park, a mountain-climbing area with huts and signposted paths. Alternatively, you can turn left in Omiš off the Adria-Magistrale, near the bridge over the Cetina, on to a road which winds its way thrillingly up into the Mosor mountains, where forests and green mountain ridges invite you to wander. From several places along the Makarska Riviera, byroads leading upwards offer access to the rocky karst. Yugoslavian mountaineers prefer to climb the peaks of Sv. Juraj (1762 m) and Vožac (1421 m) in the Biokovo range.

Hints for your holiday

National costume

'Nema problema'

Even after several visits most foreigners know very little about the history, character and scenery of Yugoslavia. As a rule, the horizon of holidaymakers on the Adriatic coast ends, literally, at the crest of those mountain ranges which border the coast only a few kilometres away from the sunny beaches. Only by travelling through the interior can you come into contact with the many different kinds of people to be found in this multi-national state.

Yugoslavs are generally open-minded when considering their present circumstances, but the political and economic problems of the country should be discussed with the natives only by visitors who have a sound knowledge of the subject. Yugoslavs are easily hurt by remarks affecting their national pride. For example, anybody who tears up bank notes or lights cigarettes with them — and this has happened repeatedly since the onset of inflation — brings ignominy upon the country.

The light, sweet Yugoslav wines and the strong Slivovitz tempt many holidaymakers to drink too much. Anyone who drives under the influence of alcohol must expect to be severely dealt with by the police, who do not waste any time with noisy drunks; Yugoslav gaols are not exactly renowned for their comfort!

Nude bathing and sunbathing are traditional in Yugoslavia. It was the first European country to allow nudism on beaches, on many camping sites and in hotel grounds. This freedom to go about without clothes has, it must be said, been abused by some holidaymakers, who take off their clothes anywhere, sometimes even in the harbour areas, so that today signs all along the coast ask people to dress suitably. Even in the churches, many visitors in bathing trunks and bikinis seem to forget where they are.

Certainly many a holidaymaker could learn something from the mixture of serenity and optimism with which the Yugoslavs, who are undeniably plagued by problems, face up to difficulties of all kinds as they arise. This ability to improvise and stay calm can be summed up in the two words *'nema problema'* (no problem).

Where to go and what to see

North Adriatic Coast between Zadar and Šibenik

North Dalmatia — scholars dispute whether it extends as far as Senj or only begins at the Novigrad Channel in the vicinity of Zadar — offers an array of varied forms of landscape. Here you find the narrow coastal strip by the steep Velebit mountain range, with the Paklenica National Park; the wide Zadar promontory with the broad plain of Ravni Kotari stretching far inland, with bays cut deep into the shoreline with the character of inland lakes (Novigrad Lake). Here a hilly area growing vines and olives; there giant canyons, waterfalls and countless islands.

Zadar Pop. 90,000

Zadar, named Idassa by the Greeks, Jader or Jadera by the Romans, originally covered only a peninsula. Today the town has spread out from its earlier centre and now extends far inland — with modern residential quarters, factory complexes and a large refinery in the south.

The harbour is much less important as a trans-shipment port for goods than that of Split. On the other hand, Zadar is a base for daily ferries to more than a dozen offshore islands. Two marinas together accommodate 830 motor boats and yachts, and the first stage of a third marina will soon be completed, with 600 moorings in the water and on land.

Changing rulers

The design of the old town, with its network of right-angled streets which still determines the layout today, dates from the time of the Romans, who made Zadar their first base on the Adriatic and raised it to the status of a free town as early as 59 B.C. Having been fortified under the Emperor Augustus with town walls, defensive towers and gates, Zadar

Zadar

became the seat of a Byzantine governor after the collapse of the western Empire, and after the fall of Salonae (Solin near Split) it was made the capital of Dalmatia.

At the beginning of the 9th c. Zadar belonged for a short time to the kingdom of Charlemagne, but under the Treaty of Aachen (812) it was handed back to the Byzantines. Under Byzantine and later Croatian rule, Zadar was able to maintain its independence against the increasing might of Venice until, in the year 1202, the Doge Enrico Dandolo concluded an incredible deal with the knights of the 4th Crusade. The Crusaders found they could not continue and, as the price for being shipped to the Holy Lands, Dandolo demanded that they should conquer Zadar — an unequalled piece of villainy which proved to be but a dress rehearsal for the conquest of Constantinople two years later by the same Crusaders, and which finally led to the Turkish onslaught on the whole of the Balkans. Apart from the churches, Dandolo reduced the whole town of Zadar to ashes.

In 1358 it was under Hungarian-Croat rule and was sold by Ladislaus of Naples to Venice in 1409, remaining in Venetian possession until the collapse of the republic in 1797. From then onwards, apart from a brief period of French possession 1805–13, it belonged to Austria. As an isolated area on the Yugoslavian mainland it was awarded to Italy under the Treaty of Rapallo in 1920, occupied by German forces in the Second World War, and finally liberated in 1944.

📷 **Places of historical interest**
Roman times: Although the old town last suffered very badly from bombardments in the Second World War, the layout of the Roman forum, 90 m long by 45 m wide, with a temple, columned hall and basilica, can still be clearly seen. Also preserved are remains of the Roman walls, on *Trg Oslobodenja* square, parts of a triumphal arch dating from the time of the Emperor Trajan, and a 14-m-high

Sarcophagus of St Simeon at Sv. Simun

column from the forum temple (which served as a pillory in the Middle Ages); outside the town are remains of the amphitheatre and burial grounds.

Early Middle Ages: The Franconian period (beginning of the 9th c.) is marked by the most monumental building from the early Middle Ages to be found on the Adriatic coast of Yugoslavia, the 27-m-high Trinity Church, later renamed *Sv. Donat*. It was built by Bishop Donat, who acted as negotiator between Charlemagne and Byzantium, and introduced elements from the palace chapel in Aachen into its most unconventional architectural form. The church has a circular ground-plan, three apses and a gallery around the upper storey.

Romanesque: The 13th c. cathedral was erected during the first period of Venetian rule, interrupted by numerous uprisings. Although not completed until 1324, the cathedral is undoubtedly the most beautiful Romanesque basilica in Dalmatia. The three-naved *Anastasia Cathedral* (Sv. Stošija), built on the foundations of an older basilica, has a 12th c. crypt, a 14th c. sacristy, marble seats in the choir for bishop and priests (12th c.), a 14th c. ciborium above the altar and a beautiful choir stall from the 15th c. Also to be seen is a sarcophagus containing the remains of Saint Anastasia, which Bishop Donat had brought to Zadar from Constantinople in the 9th c. Another interesting building is the purely Romanesque *Church of St Christopher* (Sv. Krševan; 12th c.) not far from the gate facing the sea.

Gothic: The *Church of St Francis* (Sv. Franje) and the *Franciscan monastery* were built in the 13th c. The church was last restored in the 18th c. It has beautiful, richly carved choir-stalls, paintings by Jacopo Palma the Younger and Lazzaro Bastiani, and in the sacristy (where the Treaty of 1358 was signed,

whereby Venice ceded Zadar to the Hungarian-Croat ruler) there is a Gothic winged altar from the island of Ugljan. Also worth seeing are the treasury with a large 12th c. Romanesque crucifix, and the Renaissance cloister in the monastery.

Sv. Simun dates from the 12th c., was originally dedicated to Sv. Stjepan, and, after much rebuilding, received its present name in 1632, when the sarcophagus of St Simeon was brought here from the Church of the Assumption of the Virgin Mary. Architecturally a mixture of Gothic, Renaissance and Baroque features, the church houses a special treasure — the richly ornamented silver coffin of St Simeon, which Queen Elisabeth, the wife of the Hungarian-Croat King Louis 1 of Anjou, had made by Francesco da Milano in 1380. Weighing 250 kg, it is a superb example of the art of the Italian goldsmith in Dalmatia. The bronze angels which watch over the coffin were cast in Venice in 1647 from the metal of Turkish cannons.

16th and 17th c: Mention must be made of the *Land Gate*, built by Sanmicheli in 1543, when the Venetians fortified Zadar against the Turks. After passing remains of the Roman town-wall and the medieval wall and tower, you come to the *Square of the Five Springs* (1574), where the Zadar women still go to draw water. Also dating from the Venetian period are the town's *watchtower* (1562), now an ethnographic museum, and the 17th c. *loggia*, in which court hearings used to be held.

The Archaeological Museum

This museum on the promenade displays finds from pre-Roman, Greek and Roman times (a rich collection of Roman glass is particularly interesting), and sculptures and reliefs from the early and late Middle Ages.

Restful holidays can be had in Zadar itself, in the Borik complex, which comprises several hotels, a camping-site, park and sunbathing areas. For holidaymakers planning to hire a boat in one of the three marinas, or who are waiting for a ferry to one of the 104 islands belonging to the Zadar commune, there are several hotels in the town. Places north of Zadar, especially *Diklo*, *Petrčane* and *Zaton*, are also very suitable for a quiet holiday, as the Adria-Magistrale is some way inland. The biggest hotel and bungalow complex in this area is *Punta Skala*. Since 1989 a part of it has been set aside for naturists.

Shingle beach, partly concreted *(Borik* and *Diklo)*, suitable for children.

Rowing and paddle boats for hire.

S *Zadar* yacht club.

Heated saltwater indoor pool: Hotel *Novi Park*, Borik.

Hotel *Barbara*, Borik; Hotel *Kolovare*, Hotel *Zagreb*.

Hotel *Park*, Hotel *Adriana*, Borik.

Walks from *Borik*, *Bibinje* and *Sukošan*.

Nin Pop. 2000

Here you travel through countryside vaguely reminiscent of the Roman Campagna, and which gradually becomes more and more barren. A little hill suddenly appears on your left; a few pine trees surround a tiny, ancient church *(Sv. Nikola*, 11th c.) which has a heavy superstructure like the tower of a fortress. A little further, 17 km north of Zadar, you pass through a town gate into Nin, a village of unique charm. Nothing lavish or great is to be seen here, just metre after metre of the remains of old walls, either left standing as they were or

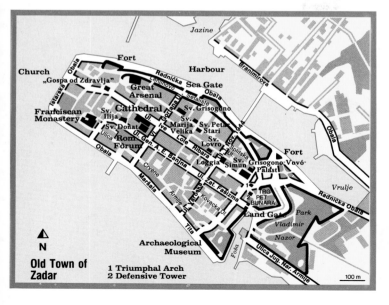

Old Town of Zadar

1 Triumphal Arch
2 Defensive Tower

N

100 m

integrated into road boundaries, houses, courtyards: remains of a great history.

Nin is a small town on a lagoon, connected to the mainland by bridges. The former peninsula was once the centre of the Illyrian Liburnia, then an important Roman free town, a regional capital in the first period of Croatian rule, the seat of a powerful bishopric and a coronation town. Here lived the contentious Bishop Gregory (Grgur), who fought on the ecclesiastical councils in support of Glagoliza, the religious language of the Croatian nation, and succeeded in pushing it through in place of the Roman liturgy. Just as in front of the Golden Gate of Diocletian's Palace in Split, so here too, on the old town square, now just a quiet village square, a mighty *statue of Bishop Gregory* by Ivan Meštrović (1883-1962) reminds us of the high dignitaries of the church. His 9th c. cathedral *Sv. Križ*, called the 'smallest cathedral in the world', is fully preserved, and stands unobtrusively and modestly behind a half-grown jungle of weeds and masonry by the side of the square.

To walk through Nin is to follow in the footsteps of its former greatness, seeking out the remains of the ancient forum, visiting the charming little museum, admiring some magnificent relics in the treasury of the parish church or simply absorbing the atmosphere of Nin's past.

Petrčane Pop. 700

11 km north-west of Zadar is a beautiful bay surrounded by pines and firs, with the twin villages of Gornje Petrčane and Donje Petrčane. Here in this tranquil, quite secluded place you can spend a very restful holiday in gentle and peaceful countryside. It is not far from here to Zadar or to the islands.

Left: Typical Dalmatian scenery

A lovely shingle beach in a sheltered bay.

 Pretty walks along the coast and to the villages of Petrčane (about 1 km).

Starigrad Pop. 100

The village of Starigrad (46 km north-east of Zadar) lies on the coast of the Velebit channel, directly below the giant mountain of the same name. Spreading to the left and right of the Adria-Magistrale, it consists of a collection of houses, restaurants, small hotels and boarding houses. Almost anyone will rent you a private room or allow campers to stay behind the house. Tourists are made welcome here in a very personal way. No wonder that the village has so many regular guests.

Shingle beach, partly concreted, and cliffs; suitable for children.

Paklenica National Park

The southern foothills of the Velebit mountains, with their wildly romantic gorges, caverns and grottos, have been declared a National Park. Paklenica National Park embraces two great canyons, Velika and Mala Paklenica, separated by a 500-m-high plateau. *Mala Paklenica* (7 km long) is reached via the village of Seline, 2 km south of Starigrad.

Tours: Information can be obtained at the National Park office, 200 m from the entrance to the Hotel *Al'an* (approaching from the north). Members of alpine clubs preparing for a tour can pitch their tents free of charge in the woods near the National Park. From Starigrad, you pass through the village of *Marasovići* to the car park at the entrance to the National Park (fee payable). To date, five routes have been marked out for walks and mountain climbs. After climbing for eight hours you reach the highest peak of the Velebit mountains, the *Vaganjski vrh* (1757 m). The route to the somewhat lower *Malovan* (1709 m) is also marked out. The main attraction of the National Park, the *Anic Kuk* gorge, some 5 km from the car park, can be reached without too much difficulty. It is two hours on foot from the car park to the *Manita peć* grotto (electric lighting is planned but it is best to take a torch with you). It is still difficult for climbers to obtain provisions. There are only two mountain huts: the Borisov Dom near the half-ruined village of Ramići (60 beds; supervised) and the unsupervised Ivine vodice (room for six to eight persons), base camp for climbing the 1751-m-high *Sveto brdo*.

Posedarje Pop. 1300
A village and small harbour at the western end of the Novigrad Sea, situated just to one side of the Adria-Magistrale road. Posedarje is a small, friendly place with a long, narrow beach. It was mentioned in the 12th c. as being a possession of the Princes of Posedarje. Visit the *parish church,* converted to the Baroque style in 1700, the Romanesque *Church of the Assumption* and the *chapel of Sv. Duh,* dating from the 15th c., on a small offshore island.

Novigrad Pop. 1000
A fishing and farming village with a small harbour in a narrow bay on the south coast of the Novigrad Sea, Novigrad is surrounded by forests of Scots pine. Mentioned in the 13th c. as Castrum, it belonged to the Venetian Republic from 1409. Above the village stands the partially preserved *fortress* (13th c.), in which Elisabeth, the widow of King Louis I of Anjou, and her daughter were imprisoned and murdered. Her shawl, which she bequeathed before her death to the ladies of Novigrad, is preserved in the *parish church*.

 Zrmanja Gorge is particularly rich in fish.

The Novigrad Sea
The Novigrad Sea, and the Karin Sea which adjoins it, are popular venues for excursions from places near Velebit and Zadar. Beyond the narrow entrance at Maslenica, between steep, yellowish cliffs, an extensive bay, called the Novigrad Sea, opens out. A romantic drive takes you through the superb Zrmanja Gorge to *Obrovac,* a small township with a turbulent past, situated up on the towering cliffs. Remains of an Illyrian-Roman settlement and of Croatian, Venetian and Turkish forts and defences are to be found in the vicinity. At the south end of the Novigrad Sea a narrow channel leads to its continuation, the Karinsko More. Worth seeing here is the little village of *Karin* with a 15th c. Franciscan monastery (restored in 1736).

Biograd Pop. 4600
Biograd lies on a peninsula, with the two deeply carved bays of Bošana and Soline to the north and south of the town. The approach road to the old coastal town goes off to the right 27 km south of Zadar. The focal point today is the 600-berth marina, directly adjoining the old town. When the yachtsmen return in the evening from the Kornati Islands, business picks up in the numerous wine-bars, inns, pizzerias, cakeshops, cafés and discos, and lasts until long after midnight. The holiday hotels, however, are situated some way away from this scene of activity.

Biograd has risen again like the phoenix from the ashes. Most probably a township of some importance grew up on the ruins of the ancient settlement of Blandona, about the year 1000. It experienced its heyday under the Croatian national leaders, and became a

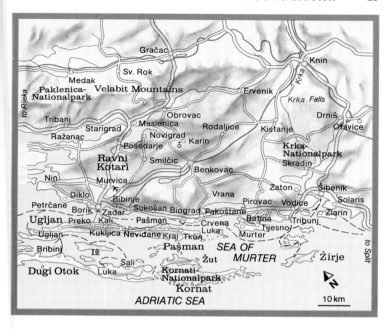

royal seat. About 1050 Petar Krešimir founded the diocese of Biograd, and in 1102 the Hungarian King Koloman was crowned here as king of Hungary, Croatia and Dalmatia. In 1125 Venetians conquered and destroyed the town, and in 1202 citizens of Zadar, fleeing before the Crusaders, settled here and named it Stari Zadar. Under Venetian rule (1409-1797) Biograd was again totally destroyed in 1646 by the Croatian occupying force, who did not want to leave it as a base for the advancing Turks. Two years later the town found a new lease of life, but without ever being able, in the course of the ensuing centuries, to regain its former importance.

There is as little to be seen now of the royal wealth as there is of the Venetian fortifications. Antique finds, and those from the old-Croatian and Romanesque period, are housed in the museum.

Beautiful bathing beaches, pretty inns and a colourful market provide a pleasant mixture of peace and lively entertainment, making Biograd one of the favourite holiday resorts in north Dalmatia.

Anyone seeking more solitude and the simple life will find in *Filipjakov* (4 km to the north) and *Turanj* (6 km to the north) two villages with lovely beaches and, of course, an ancient past. Walks in and around these two places will bring you to the remains of Roman graves, old-Croatian inscriptions, ornaments and ruins from the war-torn Venetian-Turkish period. Some 3 km to the south lies the *Crvena Luka* holiday complex: hotel and annexes, a camping-site, a harbour for boats, a suitable beach and play-areas for the children, tennis courts, non-nudist and nudist beaches.

Fine shingle beach in *Soline* and *Bošana*, partially concreted in front of the hotels in *Biograd*, elsewhere rocky.

 S Large yacht station with 7 breakwaters.

 Sandolinos in *Crvena Luka*, rowing boats for hire.

 Excursion to Lake Vrana

Lake Vrana is not one of the official excursions offered by the tourist agencies, but sometimes it is more interesting to make short trips on your own.

Driving 5 km south from Biograd along the Adria-Magistrale, you come to the northern end of the lake. Taking a road to the left near Pakoštane, in 7 km you arrive at the village of *Vrana* on the plain of the same name, one of the most fertile in Dalmatia. In the Middle Ages Vrana was a possession of Croatian rulers and princes, then the seat of the Order of the Knights Templar and of the Knights of St John of Jerusalem (12th and 14th c.). Between 1409 and 1670 it was occupied four times each by the Venetians and the Turks. Here you can marvel at the well-preserved remains of the *Maškovića han*, a Turkish caravanserai, once claimed to have been the biggest in Europe (over 50 m long and wide) and one of the rare examples of Turkish architecture in Dalmatia. *Lake Vrana*, 14 km long and 4 km wide, is the biggest inland lake in Dalmatia. It can scarcely be seen from the Adria-Magistrale, because the narrow strip between the road and the west bank is almost overgrown. Reed-covered banks and gently undulating hills in the background provide a wonderful panorama and give the lake a peaceful, slightly melancholic atmosphere. Anglers will find fresh-water fish here, especially carp and eel.

Pakoštane Pop. 1700

For countless holidaymakers, Pakoštane means the *Club Méditerranée*. About 1 km north of the fishing village of Pakoštane, an asphalt road leads off the Adria-Magistrale directly into the holiday village, which is equipped with simple straw huts for two people. Like the club's main base near Tivat on the island of *Sveti Marko,* Pakoštane is one of the simple club sites with sanitary facilities. Most of the holidaymakers here are younger people, attracted particularly by the sporting facilities. At the quay there are six boats for water-skiing, seven sailing-boats and twenty kayaks. On land, archery, aerobics and gymnastics are available. Entry to the club village is restricted, however, to those holiday-makers who are members.

 Shingle and rocky beach.

 Two starting ramps, slalom course, competitions.

  *Kozarica* holiday complex.

Pirovac Pop. 1600

As you enter the village of Pirovac from the north the approach road to the Miran naturist hotel and bungalow site branches off on the right. There are bungalows, a shady pebble beach and a shopping centre. The road to the village diverges to the right beyond the new residential quarters. Pirovac has a small harbour with a good beach and several small bays. In the Middle Ages it was owned by the diocese of Šibenik; in the 17th c. part of the populace fled to the nearby island of Murter. Remains of the *defensive wall* dating from the year 1505 are still preserved. The *parish church* (1506) was rebuilt in the Baroque style in the 18th c.

 Pebble and rocky beach.

 Boats for hire.

Vodice Pop. 5000

Like so many places on the Dalmatian coast, Vodice was once a picturesque fishing village. Narrow lanes do indeed still lead down to the waterfront, but today the ACY nautical centre dominates the scene with a marina providing over 400 berths. On the side of the road which faces the sea the souvenir stands are crowded together, and on the opposite side there are numerous guesthouses. Because of the oil film on the water caused by the large number of motor boats, you are advised not to swim in the sea but only in the hotel swimming pools.

Historically, Vodice is one of the few coastal places which were spared by the Turks. In spite of many attacks they were not successful in seizing the town, which was well fortified in the 16th c. with walls and defensive towers.

 Shingle beach, partly concreted. There are some quiet bathing bays north and south of Vodice.

 Motor and rowing boats, sandolinos.

 Hotels *Imperial, Olympia* and *Gloriette* family villas.

 Hotel *Olympia*.

 Hotels *Imperial* and *Olympia*.

 Terrace for dancing at Hotel *Imperial,* several discotheques.

In the Hotels *Olympia, Punta* and *Gloriette* family villas.

Lovely walks in the town, along the shore and to *Tribunj* (3 km), a former fishing village.

Šibenik Pop. 50,000

Šibenik is a town with three very different faces. Firstly it is a town of factory chimneys, the pall of smoke from which can be seen from afar. Secondly it is regarded as a health resort with its modern and sports-orientated hotels on the Zablaće peninsula, even though the chimneys can still be seen from there. The most beautiful face, however, is that of the old town, which is best explored on foot.

In fact, Šibenik does not lie on the sea, but rather at the mouth of the river Krka, which here forms a semi-closed harbour basin before it enters the Adriatic through the 2.5-km-long Sv. Ante channel. The town sits on a steep hill, overlooked by the three mighty fortresses of *Sv. Ana* (the oldest, and situated 70 m high), *Sv. Ivan* (125 m) and *Šubićevac* (86 m, with a terrace restaurant). The latter was formerly called 'Barone', after the Swabian nobleman Christoph Martin von Degenfeld from Eybach near Geislingen

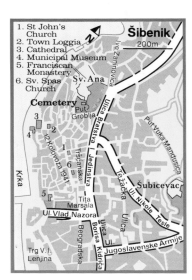

1. St John's Church
2. Town Loggia
3. Cathedral
4. Municipal Museum
5. Franciscan Monastery
6. Sv. Spas Church

in Germany, who, as a Venetian general, successfully defended Šibenik against the Turks in 1647.

To the north and south-east of the old town lies the new part, with high-rise flats and factories. After Zadar, Šibenik is the most important town on the north Dalmatian coast from an economic and cultural viewpoint, and a centre of attraction for tourists. There are wonderful views of the town, both from the sea and from the fortress of *Sv. Ana*. Viewed from the sea, it towers above you, while from Sv. Ana you gaze down upon a confusion of roofs, alleyways, steps and courtyards, and over to the sea beyond. Below Sv. Ana is a most peculiar cemetery — its terraces appear to form drawers to house the dead.

Even a stroll through the town is a rewarding experience. Palaces and splendid town houses of crumbling charm, secluded corners, well-worn steps, pillars and coats of arms set into walls, vaulted arches and protruding oriel-windows are all good subjects for keen photographers as they have both visual and historical interest.

Sunbathing at Šibenik

🐿 Croatian origins

Šibenik was founded purely by the Croatians. The town is first mentioned in 1066, in a document from King Peter Krešimirs IV. It came under Venetian rule for a short time in the 12th c., and received autonomous status from the Hungarian-Croat King Stjepan III in 1167. The kings changed continually, from Byzantine to Venetian again, then Hungarian-Croat and Bosnian, until 1412 when Venice again held sway for nearly four hundred years. Then in 1797 it was the usual story. Apart from a brief 'guest appearance' by the French, it remained Austrian until 1918, was then occupied by Italy, awarded to the kingdom of Yugoslavia under the Treaty of Rapallo in 1920, occupied by Italian and German troops in the Second World War, and liberated in 1944.

📷 Churches, monasteries and museums

St James' Cathedral. Whenever people talk about the churches of Dalmatia, the names Zadar, Trogir and Šibenik are all mentioned in the same breath. Many consider the Cathedral of St James in Šibenik to be the most beautiful. It is the masterpiece of Juraj Dalmatinac from Zadar (also known as Juraj Matin or, wrongly, as Gregor Orsini). Other master-builders also played an important part in its construction (1431 to 1555), especially Nikola Firentinac. Late Gothic and Renaissance combine harmoniously, and the wonderful building is crowned by an unusual form of roof construction, unique for the period: the main and side naves, apses and domes are vaulted with interlocked stone panels without any other means of support. On the corner pillars of the north-east apse two cherubs bear the inscription, 'These apses were built by Juraj the Dalmatian, son of Mato'. Around the outer walls of the apse is a unique portrait gallery: a line of 74 heads forms a most unusual church frieze with all conceivable types and professions assembled. Of all the beauties of the magnificent triple-naved interior, the most significant are the sanctuary, the choir gallery, the staircase to the sacristy and the baptistry which are all by Dalmatinac and Firentinac.

The Town Square, opposite the north front of the cathedral, is framed by the *Town Loggia*, once the seat of the town council (school of Sanmicheli; built 1523 to 1542, restored after the last war), and on the east by the *Small Loggia*. A fountain gives the finishing touch to the Venetian atmosphere.

Also worth seeing are the *Franciscan Monastery*, 14th c., with a 17th c. richly carved, coffered ceiling and a worthy collection of incunabula, the *Church of St John* and its elegant external staircase by Ivan Pribislavjić (15th c.), the *Orthodox Parish Church* with a

The Krka Sea at Šibenik

Šibenik Market

particularly beautiful bell-tower and darkly glowing icons inside, the Gothic *Church of St Barbara* (church museum), the churches of *St Laurentius* and *St Dominicus* and the so-called *New Church.* On the coastal side, adjoining the cathedral, is the old *Bishop's Palace* (15th c., late Gothic courtyard) and the *Rector's Palace,* today a municipal museum.

The big tourist centre of *Solaris* lies 5 km to the south on the Zablaće peninsula. This magnificently planned hotel village possesses almost every facility for sport, games and entertainment that you could wish for.

 The beach (shingle, rocks, partly concreted) and the Šibenik bathing complex can be reached by boat from the harbour *(Jadrija* and *Martinska)* in 10 to 15 minutes.

   Sandolinos.

 Surf-board hire.

  In Solaris.

 9 tennis courts at the Solaris hotels, and also badminton.

Hotel *Ivan* (Solaris). The indoor swimming pool is of Olympic dimensions for water-polo training. The hotel also has its own institute of Thalasso-therapy. Here, under specialist supervision, orthopaedic problems are treated with the latest equipment.

A supervised kindergarten in the Solaris hotel complex; children's playground and a man-made flat pebble beach.

At the beginning of July, a big *children's festival* in Šibenik, in which the whole town takes part, processions and events in the town square. Šibenik *summer festivals* (June/July) with readings, concerts and folk music and dancing performances.

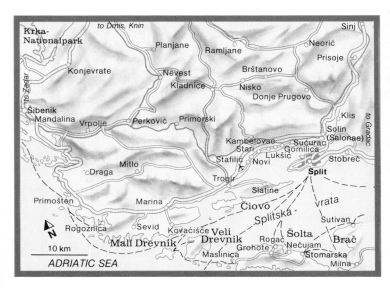

Regular events (high season) in the Solaris hotels.

 On the *Trtar*, 496 m.

A trip to Knin

Anyone who is curious to see something of the interior, and who is not put off by a trip of 60 km, should make an excursion to Knin via Drniš (33km). 10 km to the east of Drniš is *Otavice,* where the sculptor Ivan Meštrović was born and where his mausoleum can be seen. *Drniš* displays some notable remains from the Turkish period: ramparts, a mosque converted to a church, and the only preserved minaret in Dalmatia.

Knin was a strongly fortified town under the Croatian feudal lords about the 10th c. In spite of some fierce struggles against the Venetians and Turks the giant fortress is still well preserved (very attractive views all around). The *folk museum* in the Franciscan monastery has a noteworthy collection of old-Croatian art. National costume can still be seen on market days (embroidery and lace are good buys).

Coral islands

You can go by boat to the so-called coral islands of *Zlarin* and *Krapanj,* where men have fished for coral and sponges

since olden times. On Krapanj there is a small coral-grinding works and a sponge refinery.

Primošten Pop. 1600

The little peninsula, connected by a dam to the mainland, stretches out like an inquisitive, cheeky tongue into the sea, 28 km south of Šibenik. There is a little cluster of houses on the hillside and a church tower at the top. The island-hill is Primošten: it lies there enchantingly, nobody could have invented anything so pretty. To the north is a further peninsula, covered with forests of Scots pine and with a beach around it; here stands the hotel complex from where

there is a beautiful view of Primošten. To the south lies a wide bay, in the bend of which is a naturist hotel.

The vine-growing and fishing village came into being at the time of the Turkish attacks, connected to the mainland by only one bridge. Hence came its name (*primoštiti* – to bridge over). Its fortifications were razed during the 19th c., and there is nothing left to remind us of the hostilities and to disturb the tranquil atmosphere.

Shiny stone steps, bright stone-built houses with red roofs and dreamy corners radiant with flowers all invite you to linger awhile and sample the delights of the appetising food and drink.

Primošten

At Primošten

If you are not satisfied with such pleasures, you can take to the road and discover the island. It does not take long. From the *parish church*, renewed in 1760, there is a wonderful view.

 Pebble, partly concreted, and rocks.

 Adriatic hotel complex, with the renovated hotels *Zora* and *Slavec*.

In the nearby hamlets.

A special tip

The deliciously prepared sea-food in the Vila Fenc restaurant is excellent. Choose a fresh lobster or crayfish from the salt-water pool. With luck, you may even obtain some rare stone-boring mussels. On the shady terrace, above the deep-blue sea, these epicurean delicacies, with which a bottle of Babič goes down well, provide an unforgettable experience.

North Dalmatian Islands

Off the coast of North Dalmatia is a triple string of islands and islets. Many are uninhabited, and are favourite destinations for tourist excursions from the mainland. Some are slowly developing into regular holiday resorts for those seeking peace and quiet or for sports enthusiasts. The most important islands are described below.

Pag island

After Krk and Cres, Pag is the third largest Kvarn island, but it is often included in the North Dalmatian group of islands. Pag has a surface area of some 285 sq. km, is almost 60 km long, and varies in width from 2 km at its narrow, north-western extremity to 30 km in its southern part which has deeply-indented bays. Separated from the coast by the 3-km-wide Velebit Channel, in the south-east it is only 300 m from the mainland, with which it is linked by a wide-spanned bridge.

You really must see this stone monster of an island: this floating desert, which appears to rise from the sea like a mirage. It seems impossible that people can live here, but they do. In the interior, vines, vegetables, fruit and olives grow in the hollows of the valleys and in narrow fields. Salt-mining, sheep-rearing, occasional bee-keeping and fishing provide a living for the 10,000 or so inhabitants. Pag has a distinct Mediterranean climate. Sea winds (*Maestral* and *Burin*) moderate the scorching heat. The feared, cold *Bora*, which sweeps over from Velebit, occurs mostly in the spring. Pag was populated in prehistoric times by Illyrian Liburnians (remains of fortifications and graveyards near Kolan and Novalja). The Romans erected defensive positions in Cissa, now *Caska* (remains can be seen in the water when the sea is calm), Novalia *(Novalja)* and *Košljun*. The largest settlement was Pagus (Pag). The subject of a dispute between Rab and Zadar when under Croatian rule, Pag fell into Venetian hands in 1409, and from 1797 it shared the fortunes of Dalmatia, being in turn under Austrian, French and Italian domination. In 1945 the island was liberated by the Partisans.

Pag is connected by a bridge (turn off at Posedarje, 25 km from Zadar), also by car ferry between Jablanac and Stara Novalja (4–6 times daily), and between Karlobag and the town of Pag (3–6 times daily).

The town of Pag Pop. 2500

The economic centre of the island is the town of Pag. It lies between the bay of the same name and the salt-pans (annual production 12,000 tonnes), the only sea-salt extraction plant on the Adriatic coast of Yugoslavia. East of the harbour the town with its 16th and 17th c. houses rises gently up the pale yellow slopes. In the western part of the bay is a long shingle beach.

Pag lace is famous. Today you will still find women sitting in their doorways, producing delicate lacework with fine and complicated patterns of almonds, leaves and rosettes.

In all probability, the town is indebted for its first buildings, begun in 1443, to the famous Juraj Dalmatinac (see page 13), to whom the *Prince's* and *Bishop's Palaces* are also attributed. Right-angled streets lead to a large, central square, the extent of which is unexpected. In the restored and unadorned façades of both palaces can be seen Gothic windows and the remains of coats of arms. Only a Renaissance portal, which leads from the main street to the inner courtyard of the Prince's Palace (today a department store), is completely preserved. Opposite is the *parish church*, a three-

Pag

naved basilica with styles characteristic of Romanesque, Gothic and early Renaissance.

Old Pag — today the deserted town of *Starigrad* – lies some 3 km to the south, on the site of the ancient Pagus. Parts of the medieval walls, the 14th c. parish church and ruins of a 16th c. Franciscan monastery are preserved.

Novalja Pop. 2000

Novalja, originally a small fishing village, entices you to stroll and shop. On the harbour quay are six inviting bars with green roofs. Cars are left here, because the village can only be explored on foot. Villas, holiday homes and bungalows have shot up around the old centre of Novalja. Further out, in a little forest of Scots pines, lies a huge camping-site with a fenced-off naturist section. On the other side the road continues along the bay to *Stara Novalja*, a modern holiday centre with houses owned mainly by city dwellers from the interior of Yugoslavia.

In ancient times Novalja was the port for the Roman town of Cissa (now *Caska*), which was destroyed in an earthquake in A.D. 361. There is a well-preserved Roman water system (*Talijanova buža*), traces of early Christian basilicas and remains of a pre-Romanesque church from the 9th/10th c.

 The flat bays of *Pag, Novalja* and *Caska*, with shingle and rocky beaches, are suitable for children.

 Freshwater fish in the *Velo blato*.

Rowing and paddle boats for hire in *Pag*.

In addition to the delicious fresh fish dishes of all kinds (*Novalja* arranges very popular scampi evenings), there is lamb grilled or roasted on the spit, also Dalmatian raw ham, the famous Pag sheep's milk cheese and light sweet wines of the country.

Every year, from July 26th– 29th, a folk festival is held, the *Pag Summer Carnival*, in which the whole population takes part.

There are regular *folk evenings* in Pag with folk-dancing: Po paški (in the Pag manner) and Po starinski (in the old manner); and in Novalja Po naški (in the modern manner).

Every evening there is music for dancing in the Hotel *Bellevue*, Pag, and in the restaurant on Pag beach.

Extensive walks in the karst hills south-east of Pag to the *Sveti Juraj* (263 m) and further, via the mountain ridges, to the *Velebit Channel;* or you can go to the *Sveti Vid* (north-west about 8 km, 348 m), from which there is a wonderful view over the near and distant islands. Stout footwear is essential, and, so as not to be exposed to the worst of the heat, you should set off early.

Tours of the island

To the individual places on the island by bus or boat.

To the *Velo blato* lake (1 km long in summer, 5 km in winter) on the central southern tongue of the island. The lake

By boat from island to island

is surrounded by giant reed-beds, is rich in fish and a good feeding-ground for water fowl and moorhens.

To the islands off the west coast, the so-called seventeen little islands, which are more or less deserted, with only some 7000 inhabitants in all; *Maun, Olib, Silba, Premuda, Škarda, Ist* and *Molat* are the largest, in parts with beautiful forests, vineyards and olive groves. Silba, Olib and Molat, in particular, have narrow beaches of fine shingle, and Silba also has a naturist beach. Everywhere there is plenty of opportunity for historical exploration, for most of the islands were colonised in the Roman period.

Dugi Otok

Since 1985 cars have been allowed to drive on this long island, but road conditions are really only suitable for cross-country vehicles. There are hotels in *Božava* and the capital of the island, *Sali*. The side of Dugi Otok which faces the mainland has some lovely bays, while the side facing the sea is, for the most part, steep and inaccessible.

Božava Pop. 300

Božava is a good place for lovers of water sports. The diving school is run by the Association of German Diving Tutors, and issues a recognised certificate on completion of the courses.

 Car ferry (once a day) and ship (once a day) from *Zadar* to *Božava*.

 Hotel *Lavanda*, Hotel *Kadulja*, Hotel *Palma*.

Sali Pop. 1300

The name comes from the salt works which used to be in the vicinity. Worth seeing in this typical fishing village is the *Church of the Assumption* (Baroque altar with early Renaissance painting added later). There are gravestones around the church, with Glagolitic inscriptions, and remains of Illyrian defensive walls nearby.

 Hotel *Sali* with diving school, 300 m outside the village.

Luka Pop. 200

Fishing village on the east coast. There are also prehistoric finds in the vicinity, and a pre-Romanesque church to the north-east of the village.

Rock and shingle beach (*Luka*), a large bay for bathing opposite Božava in *Soline*. Naturist beaches at *Sali* and *Božava*.

  Best in *Sali*.

Kornati National Park

Over an area of 302 sq. km, 109 islands, islets and rocky reefs make up this national marine park, which was the first of its kind when it was set up in 1980. The biggest island is *Kornat*, 32 sq. m, and the second largest is *Žut*, 14.8 sq. m. All the Kornati islands 'swim' like greyish-green specks in the sea. There are large ones and small ones, many linked with each other by tongues of land, many separated by straits; and some with lakes of dark blue in the interior. On the side facing the open sea there are often steep rock-faces, rising to as high as 100 m, holding back the onrushing waves. Natural channels lead from the sea into bays where, centuries ago, fishermen and their boats took refuge in bad weather. They built wells there to obtain fresh water, and tourists today can still drink from them.

Until recently the islands were uninhabited in winter. This has now changed, and you can visit at least two of the islands out of season: on Žut there are small holiday homes and a

restaurant which is the summer rendezvous of yachtsmen; and on Kornat, where the administration centre of the national park is housed in the 'capital' Vrulje, there are quite a number of holiday homes. There are also radio stations on these two islands.

Holidaymakers who stay on the Kornati islands during the season receive supplies by ship two or three times a week. Visitors who have arrived at Murter and who have rented a holiday home on one of the islands can be taken out by cutter once a week. There is, admittedly, no mains electricity in the accommodation, but the refrigerators run on gas. The water, which is stored in cisterns, is pure.

You have to pay a fee to go boating in the Kornati National Park. Within the central and peripheral protected zones there are numerous restrictions. You need a licence to fish, and diving with oxygen cylinders and underwater photography are prohibited. Camping overnight in the open is allowed only in certain bays.

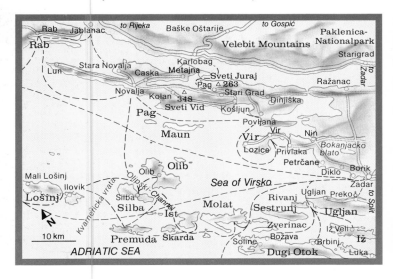

Kornati National Park

Kornati National Park

Iž island

Iž is a small island (scarcely 20 sq. km) between Dugi Otok and Pašman, surrounded by ten more, even smaller, islets. Off the harbour and main town of *Iž Veli* lies *Rutnjak* like an island park, with a dense forest of Scots pine and a beautiful bay for bathing. The inhabitants of Iž Veli are the only ones in north Dalmatia to make pottery. There are remains of Illyrian-Roman sites near Iž Veli and throughout the island.

 Car ferry (once a day) from *Zadar* to *Iž Veli*.

 Hotel *Korinjak*.

Ugljan island

Directly outside Zadar's front door, so to speak, and separated from the mainland by a narrow channel, stretches the elongated island of Ugljan, which is thickly populated. It is steep and almost inaccessible in the south-west, whereas the north-east coast falls gently away to the sea. The highest points are Šćah (288 m) and Vela Glava (238 m). Olives, vines, fruit and figs are cultivated in the fertile eastern part. Inhabited since the Neolithic Age, in the north-west in particular numerous remains of ancient buildings from the Roman period have been found. The villages were founded in the Middle Ages, and all face the coast. The island can be reached by the car ferry, which plies several times a day between Zadar and Preko.

Preko Pop. 1600

Preko is a harbour and the largest place on the island. There is a small 12th c. Romanesque church, and above the village stands the great medieval fortress of *Sv. Mihovil* (265 m), built in the 13th c. It provides a magnificent view of the whole island group. Off Preko lies the islet of *Galovac* with a Franciscan monastery.

 Hotel *Preko*.

Ugljan Pop. 1200

The most interesting building is a *Franciscan monastery* (15th c.) on the cape to the north-west of the harbour. The cloister with Romanesque capitals is worth seeing. In the vicinity are remains of a Roman *villa rustica* (country house), a prehistoric fortification and, at *Mulin* (2 km away), the ruins of an early Christian building complex (4th–6th c.) with memorials, a cemetery basilica and mausoleum.

 Hotel *Zadvranka*.

 Rowing and paddle boats for hire.

Lukoran Pop. 1700

A farming and fishing village, mentioned as far back as the 11th c. There are building remains and graves from Roman times, and a small 11th c. church with cemetery, rebuilt in the 17th c. Swimming pool on the beach.

Kali Pop. 1900

A fishing village, 3 km south-east of Preko. A road leads from Kali to the south-west coast of the island, with the deep bays of *Lamjana Vela* and *Lamjana Mala*. 17th c. Baroque church.

Kukljica Pop. 800

A small village in the south of the island. Swimming pool in a Scots pine forest on the Zaglav peninsula.

 Shingle beaches near Preko, in *Mulin* bay near Ugljan, in *Lukoran*, south-west of Kali, and near Kukljica.

 In *Preko*.

Pašman island

In the south-east, Pašman island is adjacent to Ugljan, separated only by a narrow channel, which is crossed by a bridge. On the mainly unplanned, fertile east coast lie the main villages of Nevidane (Nevidschane), Pašman, Kraj and Tkon. Illyrian graves and Roman finds confirm that there were early settlers (Pašman, Nevidane and Banj). In 1050 the island was owned by the bishopric of Biograd, and from 1126 it was in the possession of the arch-bishopric of Zadar. At the time of the Turkish attacks, refugees from the mainland settled here.

The village of Pašman Pop. 500

Houses and a small harbour on a peninsula. In the *parish church* (extended in the 18th c.) there are two late-Gothic processional crosses. The medieval *Church of St Roche* is to be found in nearby *Mali Pašman*.

Tkon Pop. 800

A former fishing village opposite Biograd. On the mountain of Čokovac north-west of Tkon stands a Romanesque *Benedictine abbey*. After renovation in the 14th c. it became a custodial home for Glagolitic literature. In the monastery church (1367–1518) is a 15th c. Gothic crucifix; there are Glagolitic inscriptions in the refectory.

Kraj Pop. 350

A small village, surrounded by olive groves. There is a *Franciscan monastery* with a 14th c. church, partly converted to the Baroque style.

Nevidane Pop. 600

Nevidane was named after an early medieval monastery of St Neviana. It has a lovely sea-water swimming pool.

 Shingle and rock beach, pretty bathing bays at *Tkon*, *Pašman* and *Kraj*.

Murter island

Murter is hardly an island any more; a bridge near Tijesno, 10 km south-west of Pirovac, joins it to the mainland. The villages of *Tjesno, Betina* and *Murter* are connected to each other by good roads (hotels in Murter and Tjesno). The marinas at Murter, Hramina and Jezera are the main departure points for cruises in the waters of the Kornati National Park. Workshops, cranes and moorings line the former fishing port, now extended into giant marine parks. Villas and imposing holiday homes, leased privately by local people, are a sign of the prosperity which the owners of the numerous yachts and boats have brought to the island.

 Almost unlimited facilities for bathing along the lavishly equipped side of the island which faces the mainland. Especially suitable for children are the flat shingle beaches near *Murter* and *Tjesno*.

 In *Tjesno* and *Murter*.

Central Dalmatia

Central Dalmatia is dominated by two towns, Trogir and Split, and the Makarska Riviera, a 60-km stretch of beach below the chilling mountain massif of Biokovo, which gives this section of the coast its unique charm, so rich in contrasts. Central Dalmatia extends from Rogoznica to Gradac in the south; the Central Dalmatian islands of Hvar and Brač have long been known as holiday resorts.

Split Pop. 260,000

Split is the capital of Dalmatia, an economic, cultural and tourist centre. After Rijeka, this pulsating and lively city has the second largest harbour in Yugoslavia. Not only does Split lie geographically in the middle of the Dalmatian coast, it is also the centre of Dalmatia in other ways, not least because, in the words of E. Maury (1896), 'If it were necessary to find that piece of European scenery most suitable for reawakening in a friend a true sense of history, I would, without any hesitation, bring him to Split.' Split can be described as the complete history of Dalmatia concentrated into a limited space, the visible and tangible embodiment of time. Split, which owes its existence to an imperial gesture, is fascinating.

History of the Dalmatian capital

Before Emperor Diocletian built his palace here at the end of the 3rd c., there already existed the Illyrian-Greek settlement of Aspalathos in the sheltered bay of the peninsula near Salonae. After his death, the great building remained in the possession of the Roman emperors. State-run weaving mills were installed in the northern half, while the living quarters in the southern section served as places of exile for emperors and their families.

After the fall of Salonae at the beginning of the 7th c., its inhabitants took refuge behind the well-fortified walls. The palace then became a middle-class town, the new seat of the diocese; the imperial mausoleum became a cathedral and the Temple of Jupiter a Christian baptistry. Under Byzantine rule until 1105, and then part of the Croatian kingdom, Split attained great economic importance as trade flourished in the 12th and 13th c. The palace walls became too restricting, so a new part of the town grew up on the

western side (around the *Narodni Trg*), and new walls were erected, remains of which can be seen to the north and north-west of the palace.

During the period of Venetian rule from 1420 to 1797, especially after the fall of Klis in 1537, prosperity declined under the increasing threats from the Turks. Epidemics of plague and cholera decimated the population. The Venetians erected a new defensive system, of which the *Hrvojeva kula* tower, south-west of Preporoda Square, remains. In the second half of the 17th c. the city recovered, and the farming

settlements of *Veli Varoš* and *Lučac* came into being on the west and east sides.

From 1797 until 1918 Split, like the other Dalmatian towns, was ruled by Austria (apart from the brief appearance of France from 1805–1813), and it became Yugoslavian in 1918. Between the two world wars the city extended still further, to the Marjan slopes in the west and to Bačvice in the east.

Sights of Split

It is the Palace of Diocletian, one of the most important examples of late-Roman

Split

architecture, which is the very core and symbol of the city, the first place tourists head for. However, Split is more than just the palace; there are also modern housing developments, large industrial sites and dockyards. Furthermore, Split is the focal point for ferries, coastal ships and cruisers.

The *Marjan* covers the western point of the peninsula. It is a big recreation park with open-air swimming pools, an oceanographic institute with a marine aquarium (open daily from 8 a.m.– 7 p.m.), a natural history museum and zoological gardens (open daily from 8 a.m. until sunset) and a four-storeyed hermitage of narrow proportions, hewn out of the rock face. The mountain overlooking Split, which is also called the Marjan, is of course part of this park. You can easily reach the peak (175 m) and the terrace restaurant (124 m) by car or on foot. The city lies at your feet, with the outline of the palace clearly standing out.

The Palace of Diocletian

The ground-plan is simple. The irregular rectangle of the palace, which today

Roman Gate, Split

contains the old town with over 3000 inhabitants, is divided by two main streets running east to west and north to south, which makes it easier to get your bearings. They meet in the centre, the peristyle, and lead to the gates: in the south to the *Bronze Gate,* now hidden in the houses built up around it, and which at one time formed a direct entrance from the sea to the *supporting vaults,* which you must be sure to see because they give the best impression of the way in which the imperial chambers above were arranged; in the east to the *Silver Gate* opposite the market and the Dominican church; in the north to the *Golden Gate,* the most magnificently designed of all, because this was the land gate and from here the road led to Salonae.

The north wall and gate are the best preserved. In front of the gate is a monumental statue of Bishop Grgur Ninski (see page 27) by Ivan Meštrović; to the side of it are a bell-tower, remains of the *Arnerius Chapel* (school of Dalmatinac) and foundations of the *Church of St Euphemia,* forming part of the complex of a Benedictine nunnery.

To the west the main street leads across to the *Iron Gate,* in front of *Narodni Trg* square, the centre of the public life of the city in the Middle Ages, with the *City Hall,* a Gothic building dating from the 15th c. (the upper storey was restored in 1820). Anyone who does not wish to join a guided tour will devise a way of exploring the palace, through the maze of narrow streets, steps and corners, sooner or later arriving at the *peristyle,* the breathtaking, open hall of pillars, the forecourt to the imperial residential quarters. In the south is the *protyron,* through which you enter the *vestibule,* the former dome-vaulted and mosaic-floored ante-room and reception hall of the emperor.

Right: Café in the Palace of Diocletian, Split

East of the peristyle stands the *Cathedral of St Domnius,* at one time *Diocletian's Mausoleum,* an octagonal building surrounded by a colonnade (peripteros). In the 13th–16th c. the five-storeyed *bell-tower* was added (the tower was entirely rebuilt at the end of the 19th c.); there are 13th c. reliefs on the interior wall. In the 7th c. Archbishop John of Ravenna had all heathen symbols removed from the mausoleum. The round inner room with two rows of Corinthian columns, and a frieze with the medallions of Diocletian and his wife Prisca, was preserved mainly in its original form, apart from a desecration of the altar to the east in the 17th c. The cathedral's greatest treasures are the wonderfully carved *wooden door* by Andrija Buvina, the stone *pulpit* and very beautiful carved *choirstalls* (all 13th c.), as well as the *Anastasius Altar* by Juraj Dalmatinac (1448) with the relief portraying the 'Scourging of Christ'. Above the 17th c. *high altar* is a Gothic wooden crucifix dating from the 14th c.

At the eastern end of the peristyle stands the former little *Church of St Roche,* now a tourist office, in which a very detailed model of the palace is on display. Today, in the basement of the palace, gold, silver, filigree and coral glisten brightly in the dark on the jewellery souvenir stands. It requires a sound knowledge of materials to be able to pick a bargain in the poor light.

In front of the Palace of Diocletian, the former main street, lined with palm-trees and splendid herbaceous borders, is now closed to vehicles. This has produced a quiet haven between the harbour basin and the palace. The impressive picture is rounded off by the nostalgic sight of sailing-ships anchored along the quay near the precincts of the old town.

West from the peristyle, a narrow lane leads to the *Temple of Jupiter,* now a baptistry, open only for guided tours. The walls, entrance and the coffered barrel-vaulting have remained unchanged. Around the font are

1 Porta Aenea (Bronze Gate); 2 Basement vaults; 3 Vestibule; 4 Peristyle; 5 Mausoleum (cathedral); 6 Temple of Jupiter (baptistry); 7 Porta Ferrea (Iron Gate); 8 Porta Argentea (Silver Gate); 9 Porta Aurea (Golden Gate); 10 Palais Papalić (Municipal Museum); 11 Palais Agubio; 12 Palais Cindro; 13 Narodni Trg; 14 City Hall (Ethnographic Museum); 15 Palais Karepić; 16 Palais Cambj; 17 Trg Preporoda; 18 Palais Milesi (Marine Museum); 19 Hrvojeva Kula defence tower

Red = Roman walls

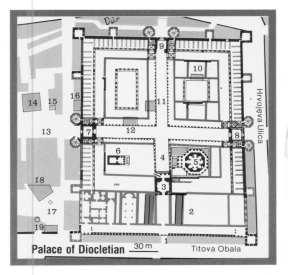

Palace of Diocletian   30 m   Titova Obala

Decorative capital in the cathedral, Split

pre-Romanesque plaques in relief, with interlaced ornamentation and the representation of a Croatian king. In the temple you will find the sarcophagi of the first archbishop of Split, John of Ravenna, and Archbishop Laurence (11th c.), as well as a statue by Meštrović of John the Baptist.

Churches, palaces and museums
In the palace is the tiny church of *St Martin* (above the north gate, with an 11th c. stone iconostasis). Along the wall over the Iron Gate is a *Chapel of the Madonna*, containing 11th c. icons and the oldest Romanesque bell-tower in Dalmatia, which dates from about 1100.

The beautiful city houses include the *Palais Agubio* with a Gothic portal and Renaissance courtyard, the 15th c. *Palais Papalić*, attributed to Juraj Dalmatinac, now the Municipal Museum and certainly the most beautiful Gothic house in the city, and the *Cindro Baroque Palace.*

In front of the Iron Gate stands a 16th c. *bell-tower*, near the city hall is the *Renaissance palace of Karepić,* and in the north-east corner of the square is the

Palais Cambj (15th c.). North-west of the Narodni Trg you will find the Renaissance cloister of the *'de Taurello' Monastery of the Madonna,* and the little Gothic *Church of the Holy Ghost.* To the south are the little *Papalić Palace,* and the Baroque palaces of *Tartaglia* and *Milesi* (the latter at the Trg Preporoda with the statue of the poet Marko Marulić by Ivan Meštrović).

The *Franciscan church* and *friary* near the Square of the Republic contain the graves of Archdeacon Tomas and the poet Marko Marulić.

In the north-eastern part of the bay of Poljud, further outside the city, are the *Poljud church* and *monastery.* In the church and the monastery's treasury there are valuable pictures by Palma the Younger, Girolamo, Francesco di Santacroce and Lorenzo Lotto.

The museums worth visiting include

Split

Split

the following: the *Archaeological Museum* in the Zrinsko Frankopanska ulica (open daily from 8 a.m.–1 p.m. and 4–6 p.m. except Mondays, and on Sundays from 10 a.m.–noon), the *Municipal Museum* in the Palais Papalić (8 a.m.–1 p.m., Sundays 10 a.m.–noon), the *Ethnographic Museum* in the city hall (9 a.m.–1 p.m., Sundays 10 a.m.–noon), and the *Meštrović Gallery* on the Marjan (daily 10 a.m.–7 p.m.).

Shingle beach, partly concreted, near the hotels and swimming pools, rocky in parts on the Marjan. The Hotel *Duilovo* has a particular attraction: the only beach-lift to be found in Yugoslavia. Split itself is hardly the place for a seaside holiday, for, within a radius of at least 3 km to the north and 10 km to the south around the harbour, sea-bathing is either most inadvisable or even prohibited.

Split possesses an open-air pool, and some hotels have their own swimming-pools: Hotels *Marjan*, *Lav*, *Miljevac*.

operas and concerts are presented in the municipal theatre, on particularly attractive open-air stages, in the Kaštelet Meštrović and in the peristyle, vestibule and basement of the palace (pop concerts during the season in the basement). The Split *International Festival of Light Music*, a competition between local and foreign singers, composers and orchestras, is held during the first ten days of August.

🚌 Excursions from Split

Solin (Salonae)

The name Salonae covers several towns lying close to and above one another 5 km from Split. Salonae is the most important site of Roman and early-Christian finds, the archaeological show-piece of Dalmatia, even though only a part has been excavated so far. Salonae was a Greek colony, the provincial capital of Dalmatia in Roman

to Kastela

Amphi-theatre

URBS NOVA Marusinac
OCCIDENTALIS
    Kapljuč
    Martyrs'
URBS Graves
VETUS
    Porta
Theatre Caesarea Manastirine

Basilica
Baths

URBS NOVA

ORIENTALIS

Otok Cradina

to Split

300 m

Jadro

to Trogir

Šuplja Crkva

Salonae

 `Split has three sports marinas with sailing boats and fishing boats for sport; sandolinos and rowing-boats can also be hired at the hotels.

 🏊 🎣 🎾

 There are casinos in the Hotel *Marjan* (Split) and the Hotel *Kairos* (Stobreč); Split also has a whole range of restaurants, theatres and concerts.

⚔ The Split *summer festivals*, which are held each year from June 15th to August 15th, are famous. Plays,

times and, after the death of Diocletian, it developed into the centre of early Christendom. Diocletian is said to have been born nearby — this has not been authenticated — and, during his time, some 60,000 people are thought to have lived in the town. The amphitheatre, scene of cruel executions of Christians, held 18,000 spectators. Religious places of worship were erected above the graves of the martyrs Domnius, Anastasius and Asterius. Salonae became the first Dalmatian bishopric. At the beginning of the 7th c. it fell victim to the invading Avars; its inhabitants left the town and fled to the nearby islands and into the palace of Diocletian. Connoisseurs of ancient sites may be somewhat disappointed when they see Salonae and find only fragments, outlines and vague traces but the place does, nevertheless, have atmosphere.

Klis and Sinj

After visiting Salonae, it is only 6 km to Klis, a large fortress erected in the 15th c. on the saddle of a hill (360 m) between Kozjak and Mosor which was a key position for Dalmatia during the period of danger from the Turks. When in 1537, after a siege of several months, the fortress fell into the hands of the Turks, Dalmatia's fate was sealed and only the narrow coastal strip ruled by Venice escaped Turkish domination. From the fortress there is a beautiful, panoramic view over Split, the islands and the Kaštelanska Riviera.

The road from Klis continues to Sinj (22 km), a town which lies in a fertile plain. Sinj has seen a lot of fighting. In 1715 a great battle took place against the Turks, which ended in victory for the people of Sinj. In memory of that victorious day, the so-called Alka festival has been celebrated every year since, on the second Sunday in August, with a tournament of knights in costume bearing arms of olden times. It is a great folk-festival, with everyone in the district joining in.

Trogir Pop. 8600

Trogir is a small island town and harbour at the western end of the Kaštelanska Riviera (see page 59), 27 km north-west of Split, connected to the mainland by a bridge over the narrow Trogir Channel, and with the island of Čiovo — which forms part of the newer town — by a lift-bridge. North of Trogir a minor coastal road branches off to the right from the Adria-Magistrale into the town, and then rejoins the Adria-Magistrale to the south. A few kilometres before reaching Trogir you pass on your right the extensive Medena hotel complex, and further on the cranes and factory buildings of the nearest island come into view. Then comes the only turn-off to the right leading to the old town of Trogir, which has now been closed to traffic.

Trogir, known to the Greeks as Tragurion, the Island of Goats, and called 'the treasure-chest of the arts' by the art historian Berenson, is an inhabited and living museum, one of the most beautifully preserved medieval towns to be found anywhere. The character of its townscape is largely determined by its situation.

A living museum

The Romans extended Tragurion, which they called Tragurium, into a port, which soon lost its importance as a result of the tremendous development of nearby Salonae (Solin). After the division of the Roman Empire Trogir came under Byzantine sovereignty, but in the 9th c. took the precaution of paying due tribute to the Croatian overlords. In the 11th c. it became an episcopal town, and in 1107 its autonomy was recognised by King Koloman. Almost completely destroyed by the Saracens a few years later, Trogir quickly recovered and really began to prosper. In spite of putting up resistance, it was forced to bow to the might of Venice in 1420. However, the distinctive cultural strength which the town had developed in the 13th–15th c.

View over Trogir

Trogir Old Town

in no way diminished under Venetian rule. For a long time Trogir remained a spiritual centre of Dalmatia and established close connections with the whole of Europe. Ceded to Austria after 1797, the French interregnum followed. From 1918 Trogir belonged to the kingdom of Yugoslavia; it was occupied by the Italians and Germans in the Second World War, and liberated in 1944.

📷 A walk round the old town

First walk through the northern *town gate* (late Renaissance) with the statue of the town patron, Ivan Ursini, as its centre-piece and its very heart. Around the big, open and bright square of *Narodni Trg* stands a collection of architectural gems which even the most fleeting visitor to Trogir will not easily forget. On the east side you find the *Municipal Palace* (once a royal court, 15th c., rebuilt after the Second World War), which may well have lost much of its beauty but still has an inner court-yard which is brimming over with atmosphere; to the south stands the *Town Tower,* with two figures by Nikola Firentinac. Solid and reassuring, the tower stands near the elegant 15th c. *Loggia,* once the public law court. On the west side you come to the *Palais Ćipiko* (to the south, separated by a narrow street, stands the little Palais Ćipiko which was formerly joined to the larger one by a bridge), which is conspicuous by its noble Gothic triple-windows placed one above the other. On the south side of the Ćipiko palace can be seen a beautiful portal attributed to Dalmatinac. The Ćipikos were one of the most respected and important Trogirian families. The lower rooms of the palace house the tourist bureau.

The Cathedral of St Laurentius forms the northern end of the square. It was begun in Romanesque-Gothic style in 1123, and completed with the tower in the 16th c. The outer walls are simple and undecorated, yet incredibly strong, and above them the slender, three-storeyed bell-tower stands gracefully against the sky. In the open portico, almost hidden, you can see the famous *main doorway* by the master Radovan, the most magnificent piece of Romanesque sculpture in Dalmatia. In the *tympanum* (pediment) he testifies to this in the self-confident words: 'This portal was built in the year 1240 by Radovanus, and is the best of all his work, as is shown by the statues and reliefs...' He was quite right.

To the left of the doorway, at the end of the porch, stands the *Baptistry* (1464), the *chef-d'oeuvre* of Andrija Aleši, also known for his work in Šibenik Cathedral.

The main attraction of the beautiful interior is a wonderful Renaissance *chapel*, dedicated to Bishop Ivan Ursini. He was Roman by origin, a sage, revered by the people as a miracle-worker. Nikola Firentinac and Andrija Aleši built the chapel in six years at the end of the 16th c. Light filters in through the little round windows below the coffered barrel-vaulting on to the twelve statues housed in niches around the chapel; these include lively and happy angels with torches standing in open doorways. The early Gothic sarcophagus of the bishop is flanked by two Baroque angels, looking somewhat out of place. The 13th c. octagonal stone *pulpit*, a 14th c. Gothic *ciborium* over the Baroque high altar, richly carved *choirstalls* (15th c.), the Gothic *Chapel of St Hieronymus* in the left aisle and paintings by J. Palma the Younger and native masters are some of the treasures worthy of attention. The *Treasury* is also interesting, with its ecclesiastical vessels, superb medieval illuminated scripts, and a priceless little treasure — a Gothic ivory triptych.

Sv. Barbara (9th/10th c.), an impressive, old Croatian basilica with three naves, is the oldest church in Trogir. Its entrance is completely built over and consequently easy to miss; it is immediately on your left in the lane leading southwards from the town square, opposite the little Palais Ćipiko.

The Church of St John, dating from the 13th c., stands to the south-east of the town square and is today a *church museum*. It contains Gothic crucifixes and a superbly vivid relief 'The Lamentation of Christ' by Firentinac, all of which are well worth seeing.

If you carry straight on you will come to the south side of the town, where the architecture has an exceptional unity. In front of the defensive tower and Renaissance south gate you will find the *Little Loggia*, where at one time travellers

had to wait for their permits to enter the town. Today the Little Loggia is the fish market. Behind it stand the strong walls of the *Benedictine convent*, in which the most valuable relic of the Greek beginnings of Trogir is perfectly preserved. This is the famous Kairos relief; as this is often away at exhibitions, a plaster cast of the relief is housed in the *municipal museum*, which is also worth a visit.

The Palais Lučić lies further along the coast to the west. Entrance is on the north side through a Renaissance portal in the courtyard.

The Church and Monastery of St Dominicus is a single-naved Gothic building with a portal by Firentinac; the vault of the Sobota family and paintings by Palma the Younger can be seen inside. The Renaissance cloister of the monastery contains a small, rather overgrown lapidarium.

Also worth mentioning are the *Church of St Petrus* and the façades of the

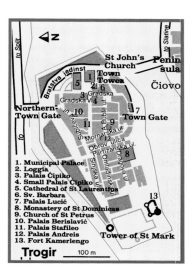

1. Municipal Palace
2. Loggia
3. Palais Ćipiko
4. Small Palais Ćipiko
5. Cathedral of St Laurentius
6. Sv. Barbara
7. Palais Lučić
8. Monastery of St Dominicas
9. Church of St Petrus
10. Palais Berislavić
11. Palais Stafileo
12. Palais Andreis
13. Fort Kamerlengo

Trogir 100 m

Fort Kamerlengo, Trogir

beautiful, even though partly ruined, *palaces of Berislavić, Stafileo* and *Andreis*.

Remains of the once strong fortifications are the embattled parapets of *Fort Kamerlengo* (13th–15th c., with an open-air stage) and *St Mark's Tower* (15th c.) which, cold and severe, stand guard on the north and south-west sides of the island.

 On both sides of Trogir, in the fertile plain, are beautiful health resorts, with hotels in *Stari* and *Seget*, some 4 km to the west; there is a regular bus service. The Hotel *Medena* near Seget offers modern amenities of all kinds, including sports facilities.

   Hotel *Medena*.

 Terrace by the sea for dancing, Hotel *Medena*.

Čiovo Island

The Island of Čiovo also has facilities for bathing. Worth seeing is the 13th c. *Monastery of Sv. Križ* (4 km east of the bridge between Trogir and Čiovo). The marvellous panorama from the Prapatnica heights (6 km on the road to the north) makes the climb well worth while.

Riviera of the Seven Castles
Pop. 12,000

The *Kaštelanska Riviera* is a rich, fertile plain stretching from Trogir as far as Split, with the soft lines of the mountain ranges of Trnošćak, Labinštica, Opor and Kozjak in the background, and enclosed like a bay by the island of Čiovo in the west and the Split peninsula in the east. It is an ideal place for a summer break. Men of means in both religious and secular spheres, from Split and Trogir, discovered this long ago, and built monasteries, country seats and fortified palaces here. Thus in the 15th and 16th c., thirteen castles gradually appeared on the shore, as people had to protect themselves against attacks by pirates and Turks; seven of these castles are still partly standing. When the Turks attacked, the inhabitants of the surrounding countryside fled to the shelter of the walls and stayed there.

Small villages arose in and around the castles, and in the course of time these have almost grown together. The city of Split has meanwhile encroached upon this idyllic scene. Two new towns have been built, Resnik and Jugovinil, and drifts of factory smoke occasionally darken the pleasant landscape.

Listed in order, from west to east, the castles are:

Štafilić: A fortified Renaissance building with a defensive tower and an 18th c. church lie a little way west of Split airport.

Novi: This has a defence tower of the former Čipiko fortress and a Renaissance chapel and loggia, dating from the 18th c.

Stari: While the northern part of the castle is strengthened by a defence tower, the south front resembles a country house. Remains of the old walls can still be seen in the village houses. There is also a Baroque parish church.

Lukšić: As well as the castle there is a 16th c. parish church with Baroque wooden altars. In the new church is an Arnerius altar by Dalmatinac. West of Lukšić are ruins of *Rušinac* castle. Near *Ostrog,* 3 km to the north, is a 12th c. Romanesque church.

Gomilica: The land was owned by the Benedictine nuns from Split as long ago as 1078. At the beginning of the 16th c. the castle was erected on an islet off the coast; the bulk of it has been preserved in its original form. There is a small 12th c. church.

Sućurac: A country house with Gothic windows. Parts of the defensive walls have been preserved. The castle itself has been converted into flats; it could be described as a miniature version of Diocletian's palace in Split.

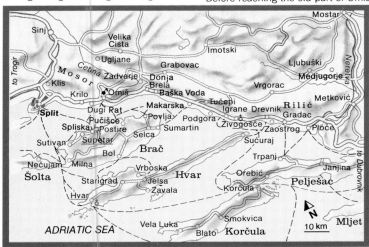 A rural atmosphere, good bathing facilities everywhere and in *Stari* and *Resnik* hotels. The proximity to Split and Trogir is a particular advantage for art-lovers.

Shingle beach, concrete and rock.

S Sailing clubs in Split, a small marina at the Hotel *Palace* in Stari.

Hotel *Palace*, Stari.

Walks along the coast and in the villages.

To the peak of the Kozjak (780 m), starting from Sućurac castle.

Omiš Pop. 4600

Before it reaches Omiš the Adria-Magistrale runs just above sea-level through villages nestling close together.

Then it swings to the left, and a massive mountain ridge comes into view, the Mosor, which falls steeply away on its western side. The Veste Starigrad, a fortress 300 m up on the mountain, overlooks the little town below. The grand, natural backdrop of Omiš — to the right the Mosor, looking as if it had been trimmed with a knife, and to the left an even higher mountain of the Poljica massif — is dominated by the estuarine channel which the River Cetina carved out for itself many thousands of years ago. Later the Cetina brought down a lot of fertile soil, which it deposited on both sides of the estuary, and which today forms the basis of the beach.

Nature favoured the little town which grew up at the mouth of the river, but modern industry has sullied this once idyllic place with a breeze-block factory at one end of town, turning the sky grey, and a cement factory at the other end, belching forth clouds of yellow dust — two classic pieces of environmental pollution which, in spite of the ideal beaches, have prevented the town from developing into a holiday resort.

Before reaching the old part of Omiš

you will pass the bridge over the Cetina.

 Pirate tradition

In Roman times the town was called Oneum; later pirates from the Neretva region to the south settled here and gained for Omiš its fearful reputation as a pirates' lair. In the Middle Ages the town was fortified and under the rule of Croatian princes. Wild and blood-curdling tales are told of its inhabitants, who for centuries led the lives of freebooters. Nobody was safe from them; not the Crusaders, whose ships they plundered, thus provoking in 1221 a Holy War ordered by the Pope; nor Venice, which needed all its strength and not inconsiderable financial resources to overcome them. It was 1444 before it succeeded. Then some of the inhabitants moved to Senj, and to their pirate colleagues and rivals in the north, where they were able to continue to pursue their bloodthirsty pirate tradition for a further two centuries.

It is pleasant to walk through the town, with its charming *square,* first to the Baroque *parish church* which has a beautiful portal and bell-tower, continuing to the *town tower,* then to the end of the main street to the 16th c. *Church of the Holy Ghost* (with a painting by Palma the Younger), and on to the noteworthy pre-Romanesque little *Church of St Petrus* (10th c.), situated on the left bank of the Cetina in the *Priko* district. Omiš has a local *museum* with a small archaeological and ethnographic collection.

 There are good facilities for bathing in Omiš itself, in *Krilo, Supetar* and *Dugi rat* in the north-west; and also in the south-east, especially in the bays of *Brzet, Mala* and *Velika Luka* (Hotels *Brzet* and *Ruskamen*), and in the quiet fishing villages of *Mimice* and *Pisak.*

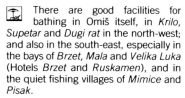 Hotel *Ruskamen;* naturist and other beaches.

 Boats for hire in Omiš, Mimice and Pisak.

 Every year, in the second half of July, Omiš organises a big *folk festival,* in which groups of singers from all over Dalmatia compete.

Into the Cetina valley

Anyone who holidays in Omiš or nearby should not fail to make a trip into the Cetina valley. The countryside is wonderful, and the first part of the journey through the rocky gorge of the Mosor is truly impressive.

If you stop on the left bank of the river, a rather stony road leads to the *Radmanove mill.* After about 6 km there is a turn on the left, which you can easily miss; and this leads downhill to the mill. Here you can enjoy some refreshment by a trickling spring and experience the simple life before taking further walks in the valley. Even in the hottest weather it is pleasantly cool here. You can also continue to the Cetina waterfalls (*Mala* and *Velika Gubavica,* 48 m), round steep bends to the village of *Zadvarje* (24 km), then downhill again to the Adria-Magistrale (8 km) and a further 8 km to Brela or back to Omiš.

You can also climb to the top of the hill from where there is a magnificent view over the Cetina gorge out to sea. The road to take branches off at the Cetina bridge, or just before it if you come from the north. First of all the road follows the river, and then, near the power station, the winding uphill stretch begins. After about 1.5 km there is a platform on the right, with a bronze statue. Further up to the right is a road leading off to a blocked tunnel, and on the left, also blocked, an old military road which led up to the coastal mountain ridge. If you carry on further straight ahead, you will immediately come to the idyllic mountain village of *Gata,* encircled by forests and meadows.

The Cetina valley

The Makarska Riviera

Brela Pop. 1400

Brela is the start of the Makarska Riviera, the most beautiful part of the Central Dalmatian coastline. Brela extends in terraces through vineyards and pine-woods along a gentle slope leading down to the sea. It has a small harbour and a town centre with a modern shopping area. Brela is not very old, and grew up as the result of an influx of people from hamlets in the Biokovo region. On both sides of Brela are beaches of fine shingle, with a few rocks dividing the string of bays. Gostionas (inns) flank the street which winds through the township, and everywhere there are flower-filled terraces, with superb views over the Adriatic and the broad ridge of the island of Brač. Brela is like a large garden, where the beautiful sunsets will enchant you as you stroll along the beach in the evening. As the beach falls away somewhat sharply into the sea, the area is not without danger for small children.

 Rowing and motor boats for hire.

 Hotel *Berulia,* Hotels *Maestral, Marina, Solino.*

 In Baško Polje (2 km away).

 Hotel *Berulia.*

 Dancing in all hotels, also afternoon tea-dances.

 Feast of St Stephen (August 3rd).

 Folk evenings every two weeks in the Hotel *Maestral.*

 To the south, on the road to *Baška Voda* (1 to 4 km, depending on where you set out from); to the north along the seaside promenade or through the village, leading to a good path in the forest; side-roads along the way take you to the Magistrale (buses to Split or Makarska).

 To the *Veliki Kuk* (585 m) in the Biokovo, a climb of about 1½ hours. A beautiful walk to *Gornje Brela* (a cemetery with Bogumil stones).

 Into the hinterland

To *Imotski* (40 km), the little town on the border of Hercegovina, at the centre of the Imotsko Polje, a broad karst plain, surrounded by steep mountains with the *Blue and Red Karst Lakes.* The road, passing through varied scenery, is stony and bumpy for a short stretch. 2 km north of Brela you drive through the Vrulja Gorge which acts as a funnel for the *Bora,* a wind which is generally strong.

Baška Voda Pop. 1400

Baška Voda is a pretty little village, 10 km north-west of Makarska. The area was inhabited way back in Roman times (graves have been uncovered near *Promanja,* some 3 km to the east), and the town grew up at the beginning of the 18th c. Baška Voda has a very lovely beach, 1 km long, lined with pine trees, and is surrounded by olive groves and vineyards. It will never outstrip Brela in popularity but as both develop they are becoming increasingly favoured by holidaymakers on the northern Makarska Riviera.

Baška Voda

Hotel *Horizont*.

 In the Hotels *Horizont* and *Slavija*.

 Folk festival on May 1st.

Lovely long walks along the beach towards Promanja or along the road to Brela (about 5 km to the town centre).

Makarska Pop. 8000

Makarska, the main town on the stretch of coast named after it, was a pleasant little fishing port a long time ago, and you will find older travel guides sing its praises. Whether you take the branch road to Makarska after turning off the Adria-Magistrale, or travel by boat, there is one striking feature — the sobering sight of the multi-storeyed hotel, which obstructs the view of the old town as you approach. Nevertheless Makarska is full of interesting corners and still completely preserved. There is lively activity in the evenings, with people parading along the promenade, countless little bars, and yachts to be seen in the harbour basin.

The early history of Makarska is not fully known. A Phoenician settlement probably existed in the dim and distant past and perhaps there was an Illyrian one as well. Muccurum, a Roman settlement, was said to have been destroyed by Germanicus in the 1st c. A.D. and by the Ostrogoth king Totila in the 6th c. In the 7th c. Slavs, Neretvan pirates, settled here, and made Makarska one of their main bases. It was under Croatian and Hungarian-Croatian rule until the 14th c. and was then held by Bosnian princes from 1324 until 1464. In 1499 they had to give way to the Turks, and the latter, in turn, to the

Makarska

Venetians in 1646. Following the collapse of the Republic of Venice, the town was under French occupation until 1815, and then annexed by Austria until the end of the First World War.

 Sightseeing

Only relatively few buildings from early times have been preserved: on the beach road there is a beautiful *Baroque house* and the *Church of St Philip Neri;* on the *town square,* with its little Venetian fountain, is the 18th c. *Parish Church of St Mark* with an overlaid marble altar, a Venetian work of art, and 16th c. icons in the sacristy. Worth seeing is the *Franciscan monastery* from the 15th c. (restored in the 16th and 17th c.), not only for its splendid bell-tower, but also because of its wonderful collection of shells, housed in the beautiful cloister and in the monastery cellar.

 A long shingle and rock beach, partly concreted near the hotels.

 Makarska sailing club.

 Rowing and motor boats for hire.

 Hotel *Dalmacija.*

 The Makarska hotels lie on both sides of the extremities of the bay and also outside the town to the north-west. You can therefore enjoy peace and quiet, and yet be only a few minutes' walk from the busy little town.

 Hotels *Meteor, Riviera,* discotheque on the harbour.

 Amor on the Sveti Petar peninsula, terrace for dancing at the Hotel *Dalmacija, Kuk* night-bar on the Tučepi road.

From July 26th to 27th there is a *fishermen's night,* similar to a folk festival.

Lovely walks through the town, along the shore and to the slopes of the Biokovo.

In the Biokovo, to the summit of *Sv. Juraj* (1762 m), a 4-hour climb, and to the *Vožac* (1421 m). The road leads north-east from the town, through Makar and the hamlet of Velo Brdo (636 m), to the *Partizan* tourist hostel (1370 m); the final part of the climb starts from here. You can also reach the tourist hostel by a metalled road, which leads from Makarska, via Old Tučepi, eastwards to the *Staza Pass* (897 m; magnificent all-round view) and then forks — to the north to the Partizan refuge; to the east via Kozica into the hinterland and Hercegovina.

Tučepi Pop. 1600

The seaside resort of Tučepi consists of several parts: a complex of hotels with their annexes (3 km south of Makarska); the former fishing village of *New Tučepi* also called *Kraj* (2 km further on); *Old Tučepi,* on the slopes of the Biokovo, and a 4-km-long shingle beach backed by a forest of pine, tamarisk and olive trees. The area was already inhabited in olden times, but was first mentioned in writing in the 15th c. The most important thing to see lies in the garden of the Neptune hotel — the little *Church of Sveti Juraj,* dating from the 13th/14th c., with Roman capitals built into it.

The shallow shingle beach is very suitable for children.

Rowing boats for hire.

 Hotel *Jadran;* a new sports centre between the Hotel

Tučepi

Neptun and the Hotel *Alga;* also cycles for hire.

 Hotels *Neptun, Alga;* and in the *Kastela* on the new promenade.

 Hotel *Jadran;* see also Makarska (regular bus service from the hotels).

 Events every fortnight in the Hotel *Jadran.*

 A beautiful road along the shore, to *Old Tučepi* (alt. 800 m) in 1½ hours.

Podgora Pop. 1300

Podgora — a small port and former fishing colony — is very beautifully situated 7 km south-east of Makarska, in a wide bay fringed by pine woods on the slopes of the Biokovo. Orange and lemon trees and gnarled olives encircle the town. The hotels, the private owners of guesthouses, cafés, pâtisseries and souvenir shops all take a lot of trouble to encourage visitors to come back again. Particularly delightful are the lovely walks along the shore which enable you to become better acquainted with the Makarska Riviera.

The large monument high above the town, known to the locals as the 'Seagull's Wing', commemorates the Partisan struggles during the Second World War.

 A narrow shingle beach, separated from the hotels by a road.

  Hotel *Minerva.*

 Hotel *Podgorka*.

Those who like genuine folk entertainment will enjoy the extensive programme of the 'Fishermen's Night' at the end of July.

Regular performances in the Hotel *Mediterran*.

To *Old Podgora*, ½ hour.

Igrane Pop. 400

The further south you go, the quieter and less influenced by tourism the places become. Igrane lies on a steep slope 18 km outside Makarska, on a small peninsula. At its highest point stand side by side the tall, slender bell-tower of the 18th c. *parish church* and a stout 17th c. *fortified tower,* built as a defence against the Turks. Narrow stone paths and steps lead you through the town, agaves grow unexpectedly out of walls, and from almost everywhere there is a wonderful view of the wide bay to the south, with its lovely shingle beach, at the other end of which stretches Živogošće. Unfortunately in recent years a number of disastrous forest fires have ravaged the area around Igrane.

Živogošće Pop. 500

A pleasant walk of scarcely 3 km from Igrane bring you to Živogošće, which comprises a cluster of several hamlets, a small harbour, a modern hotel and, not far away, an 18th c. *Franciscan monastery*. East of the monastery there is a spring, with an inscription chiselled into the rock. It is attributed to a Roman poet, who is said to have lived in a summer residence here.

 Shingle beach.

 Hotel *Nimfa*.

Zaostrog Pop. 400

Zaostrog is very picturesquely situated on the southern foothills of the Biokovo, in the Rilić mountain range, and was inhabited in Roman times. There is a Gothic *parish church*, later converted to the Baroque style, and a *Franciscan monastery* dating from the 16th/17th c.

A lovely beach, surrounded by pines and olives.

To *Drvenik* (3 km north-west, ferry to Sućuraj on Hvar); and to the villages of *Podaca* and *Brist*, all with good bathing facilities.

Gradac Pop. 1200

Gradac is the southernmost holiday resort on the Makarska Riviera. Of all the places in the vicinity, this straggling village has the biggest and most beautiful bathing beach.

Nearby are traces of a *Roman wall*, remains of old *fortifications* and a *defensive tower* built in 1661 against the Turks.

A shingle beach, 3 km long.

  SAUNA

Rowing and paddle boats, as well as surfboards, can be hired at the Hotel *Labineca*.

 Freshwater fish in the *Baćinsko* lake and *Neretva delta*.

South of Gradac the countryside changes. The mountains recede, and before it reaches *Ploče* (11 km) the road skirts the fragmented inland lake, Baćinsko jezero, and continues to the Neretva delta, with rice fields and broad areas of sedge and reeds. Car ferries leave from Ploče for Trpanj, on the Pelješac peninsula.

The island of Brač

Central Dalmatian Islands

The island of Šolta was formerly the favourite destination for visitors making excursions from Split and the surrounding area. More recently, however, the island's villages of *Maslinica, Nečujam* and *Stomarska* have slowly developed into popular holiday places, even though they are, at least temporarily, overshadowed by the tourist centres of Hvar and Brač.

The island of Šolta

Šolta (55 sq. km; pop. 3000) once formed part of the large neighbouring island of Brač. It broke away as the result of a seaquake, leaving the straits of *Splitska vrata,* a narrow channel 15 km south of Split. To the south Šolta has a steep, rugged and rocky coast, on the north side lie the two large bays, *Rogač* and *Nečujam,* and in the west — the most fertile part of the island — is a great plain with well-tended crops of grapes, mulberries, olives and rosemary.

Šolta was first mentioned in the 4th c. B.C. as the Greek settlement of Olyntha, and in the 14th c. it was described for the first time, in the statute of Split, under its Croatian name of Šolta. After the destruction of Salonae and the invasion of the Slavs, Šolta was closely linked with Split and for centuries the island was owned by the city. From the 13th to the 15th c. Šolta was frequently exposed to predatory attacks by pirates from Omiš and the Venetians. After the capture of Klis in 1537, many inhabitants from the mainland settled here.

Nečujam Pop. 500

This village, situated in the north of the

island, on the large 2-km-long indented bay of the same name, consists in the main of a holiday centre among pine woods. In Nečujam the Croatian poet Marko Marulić — his monument stands on the Trg Preporoda in Split — had a summer residence, which now houses a commemorative collection. Remains from the past are the ruins of a little 15th c. *Gothic church* and, at the eastern end of the bay, fragments of *Roman walls*.

Maslinica Pop. 650

This little fishing village, situated in a sheltered bay in the west of the island, has a small harbour, and with the little islets offshore offers particularly good fishing.

Stomarska Pop. 100

A little village on the north-east coast of the bay of the same name. Above the village stands the Baroque *Church of the Virgin Mary*, and a cemetery with fragments of an antique sarcophagus.

Shingle and rock beaches in the bathing bays at the places mentioned and at *Rogač*, north of Grohote.

Grohote

The largest settlement on the island, with remains of *Roman buildings* and *mosaics*, also a *parish church* with an altar-piece by the Flemish painter Pieter de Coster. Near the church are foundations of an *early Christian basilica* of the 6th/7th c. and a 17th c. *defensive tower*; in a field a little way away stands a tiny 14th c. *Gothic church*.

The island of Brač

Brač is the third largest, and the most heavily populated, Yugoslavian island (394 sq. km, 40 km long, 5–14 km wide; pop. 21,000). It lies off the coast near Omiš, separated from the mainland by the 6–11-km-wide Brački channel, and from the island of Hvar by the 4-km-wide

Hvarski channel. The higher areas of the island are covered mainly with black and Aleppo pines, the rest mostly with macchia bushes. The climate is mild, but is strongly influenced by the *Maestral, Jugo* and *Bora* winds. The northern section of the coast, between Povlja and Pučišća, suffers in particular from the roaring Bora. Wine, olives and fruit, especially St Lucie cherries and almonds, are the main agricultural products. Brač is famous for its marble, which was used in building the Palace of Diocletian, and the White House in Washington (there are quarries near Pučišća, Selca, Postira, Spliska, Škrip and Donji Humac). The main places on the island have regular boat services to the mainland, and there is also constant traffic between Bol and Jelsa, on the island of Hvar.

 Successive rulers

Brač was colonised in prehistoric times. Its name probably comes from the Illyrian language (Brattia is said to derive from Illyrian *brentos* – stag). Until the 9th c. the island belonged to Byzantium, then it was conquered by the Neretvans and later incorporated into the Croatian kingdom. In the 13th c. Omiš gained possession of the island, but it was snatched away again by Split in 1240. In the 14th c. Brač came under the sovereignty first of Hungarian-Croatian and then of Bosnian kings, with considerable rights of autonomy. Venice ruled from 1420 to 1797. The island retained its old privileges and the inhabitants, who had retreated into the interior in the face of the many pirate attacks, settled once more along the northern coast. Following the collapse of the Venetian Republic, Brač came under Austrian rule until 1918, apart from the brief period of Napoleonic power. Occupied by Italian and German troops in the Second World War, the island was liberated in 1944.

Brač

Sunbathing beach on Brač

Supetar Pop. 2100

Supetar is the administrative centre and main town of the island, and lies in a beautiful bay on the north coast, encircled by a thick pine forest. Supetar and the town of Bol are the most important tourist resorts. It is connected with the mainland by ferry to Split (10–15 times a day) and between Sumartin and Makarska (3–5 times a day). Supetar has no particular sights worth seeing. The *parish church* with its monumental flight of steps dates from the 18th c. and the *mausoleum* of the Petrovinać family, featured on many postcards, is not particularly noteworthy. Even so Supetar is a pleasant place for a holiday, with beautiful bathing beaches.

In the town and near the hotels the beaches are of sand and shingle, suitable for children; outside the town there are in places rocky cliffs between the individual bays. Naturist beach 3 km.

Sandolinos and rowing boats for hire.

  In the nearby sports centre.

 Boccia.

 Children's playground and baby-sitting.

🎵 *Laterna Disco;* in the Hotel *Plaza* there is music on the terrace daily from July.

🍸 *'Nono'* in the Hotel *Tamaris,* Hotel *Kaktus.*

🍴 In Postira, at the beginning of July, is the *Postirske Fraje* (folk festival, poetry reading, pop festival).

🚌 **Tours of the island**

To Spliska, a village and small harbour, 6 km east of Supetar, with a lovely bathing beach. There is a 16th c. *Renaissance castle* and a *parish church*

with some valuable paintings. Above the village are quarries which supplied the building materials for the Palace of Diocletian. In the Rasohe quarry, a *figure of Hercules* is hewn out of the rock (3rd–4th c.).

In Škrip, 2 km south of Spliska, can be found the remains of *Illyrian cyclopean walls*, a triple-naved *pre-Romanesque church*, the *Cerineo castle* (1618) and a *Baroque parish church*, with pictures by Jacopo Palma the Younger.

To Postira, 6 km to the east, which has several bays with shingle beaches. To the east of the village are the ruins of an *early Christian basilica* (5th–6th c.).

To Sutivan, where there is a beautiful beach with numerous bays, and an extensive pine forest, 7 km to the west.

To the Vidova Gora, which at 778 m is the highest point on the Yugoslavian Adriatic islands. The road leads south via Nerežišće and then climbs, with some hair-raising stretches, to the

The harbour at Spliska

summit where you will be rewarded with an unforgettable view of the coast from Trogir to Makarska, of the islands of Hvar and Korčula, and of the open sea.

Povlja Pop. 400

A fishing and farming village, with inviting bays nearby. In the village there is an *early Christian basilica* (5th–6th c.), and near the church a *castle* which has been renovated several times.

   200 m away.

  Hire of motor boats and rowing boats.

 Hotel *Galeb*.

Pučišće Pop. 1700

A fishing village and centre of stonemasonry, situated in the bay of the same name at the eastern end of the north coast. Worth seeing are some renovated *castles* and, in the *parish church*, a reredos by Palma the Younger and the altar of St Anton, a fine example of Dalmatian wood-carving. There is an extensive shingle beach.

Sumartin Pop. 600

This is a fishing village on the south coast, with a *Franciscan monastery*. Moving inland you will find the village of *Selca* with the remains of a prehistoric *fortress* nearby. In the *parish church* is a representation of Christ by Ivan Meštrović. There are several bays suitable for bathing outside the village.

Bol Pop. 1100

This one-time fishing village is today the tourist centre of the island, with many hotels and holiday complexes. The biggest attraction of the resort is the *Zlatni Rat* (Golden Horn) beach of fine shingle. As there is no through traffic, except to and from Supetar harbour, Bol is very quiet.

You should visit the *Dominican monastery* on the Glavice 'foothills', as they are known. There is a painting from the Tintoretto school over the main altar. The hotels are some way outside the town.

 In all there are 12 km of beach east and west of Bol; in the west lies the famous Zlatni Rat sandbank, which gives the appearance of moving. Behind Zlatni Rat are facilities for naturist bathing.

 At the *Borak* hotel complex, and Hotel *Bretanide*.

   Diving and surfing courses.

 Hotel *Elaphusa* (heated salt-water pool).

 Hotel *Elaphusa*.

 Hotels *Borak*, *Bretanide*, *Elaphusa*.

Beautiful walks along the shore and mountain paths towards Vidova Gora.

On the *Vidova Gora* (778 m), the ascent takes about 2½ hours.

To Murvica

A small village to the west which you can also reach riding on a donkey. Outside the village lies an abandoned *monastery* and a *church* in a grotto with pictures of fantastic figures, probably folk-art of the 15th c.

The island of Hvar

Hvar, situated between Brač/Šolta in the north, and Korčula and the Pelješac peninsula in the south, has an area of 300 sq. km, and is the longest of the Yugoslavian islands (69 km). It calls itself the sunniest island in the Adriatic,

The island of Hvar

and has been famous for a long time as the 'Yugoslavian Madeira'. Without any doubt it is one of the most beautiful islands in the area covered by this guide. A mountain range runs from one end to the other (highest point is Sv. Nikola, 626 m), the rocky south coast falls away steeply to the sea, and the north and west of the island are heavily indented, with many bays and promontories. This is where you will find the holiday resorts, all with regular boat services to Split on the mainland; there are also regular car ferries from Sućuraj on the eastern tip to Drvenik on the Makarska Riviera. Holm-oaks, Aleppo pines, rough heathland with aromatic shrubs, vines, olives, rosemary and lavender all grow in lush profusion.

One ruler after another

Hvar has been inhabited from the early Neolithic Age, and in 385/384 B.C. the Greeks founded the colony of Pharos (today Stari Grad), and probably at the same time Dimos, the present town of

Hvar

Hvar. For a short time the island belonged to the Illyrian state, before the latter succumbed to the Romans in 219 B.C. In the 7th c. A.D. Slavonic Neretvans settled here, and soon after that there followed a period of constantly changing rule: Byzantium from 870 to 886, then the Neretvans again, Croatian kings in the 11th c., Venice from 1145–64, 1164–80 Byzantium again, and the Hungarian-Croatian kings from 1180–1278. Until 1358 Hvar, under the rule of Venice, defended itself against the pirates from Omiš. Then followed Hungarian-Croatian and Bosnian kings, and finally the Ragusa republic. Venetian once more from 1420–1797, the island shared the fortunes of the coastal towns until 1918. It was occupied by Italian troops until 1922, as it was again in 1941; German occupation preceded liberation in 1944.

Walking in the Old Town, Hvar

The town of Hvar Pop. 3300

With the setting up of a hygiene society, the 'Societa Igienica', in 1868, Hvar began to develop into one of the most popular and sought-after holiday destinations in the Dalmatian area. You will notice immediately that the town is experienced in dealing with people from abroad. It is attractively situated on a largish bay in the south-west of the island, protected on the landward side by a ridge of hills. Offshore are the so-called Pitch, or Devil's Islands. An impressive broad promenade along the shore, lined with palm trees, elegant Venetian façades, inviting hotel terraces near the water, and oleander blossoms will be your first impression of the town. Immediately you feel the holiday atmosphere. People also like to visit Hvar in winter, for the climate is very mild.

It was in the late Middle Ages that Hvar first grew into a large town. It is obvious that Venice must have played a major role in its development, and that it prized the sheltered harbour as a key factor in providing winter quarters for its ships. However, Hvar was more than just a military base at that time; it was also a home for poets and artists. One of Europe's oldest theatres was installed in the upper storey of the Arsenal (1612), where theatrical and operatic performances were held until 1796. The present décor dates from the year 1803.

📷 Around the town square

The *Arsenal*, erected between 1579 and 1611, and extended in 1612 by the Venetian Podestà (mayor) who added a corn store *(fontik)* with a magnificent, large terrace, stands solidly on the south side of the *town square*. Its dark, cavernous vaults, which used to be the storehouse for the municipal gallery, are now a supermarket.

On the east side of the square stand the *Bishop's Palace* and the *Cathedral of*

Hvar harbour

St Stephen (16th/17th c.) with a beautiful, four-storeyed bell-tower and a façade which, from a distance, looks like a copy of the façade of Šibenik Cathedral. On the Baroque altars in the interior are paintings by Palma the Younger and by the 13th c. Venetian school, and 17th c. Italo-Byzantine Madonna icons. There are Gothic choir stalls and near the entrance a relief depicting the 'Scourging of Christ', clearly a variation of the relief by Dalmatinac on the Anastasius altar in Split Cathedral.

West of the town square, in the centre of which stands the great *fountain* dating from 1529, is the *Leroj clock tower,* started in 1466 and not completed until the 16th c., the sole remains of the former Podestà palace. Near the Leroj the loggia of the Palace Hotel, also called the *Sanmicheli Loggia,* is reminiscent of the former 16th c. town-lodge.

North of the square the *town walls,* begun in 1278, and leading up to the *Fortica* fortress, encompass the oldest part of the town. Here, and also to the east of the harbour, some beautiful façades of old patrician houses have been preserved. These include, near the

Backstreets of the Old Town

entrance to the town square, the unfinished *palace* of the poet Petar Hektorović, with its projecting Gothic triple-windows.

Worth mentioning are the Romanesque church of Saints *Kosmas and Damian*, the Gothic *Church of the Holy Ghost* and, outside the walls to the west, *San Marco*, of which only the façades and the splendid tower remain standing. Higher up, on a wooded hill, lie the remains of the Orthodox *Monastery of St Catharine*, over which a defensive tower was later built. Today it is an open-air theatre.

Franciscan monastery

You should leave yourself time to visit the *Franciscan monastery*, built in the 15th c. at the south-east end of the bay of Hvar (only 10 minutes from the town centre). The church, with a relief by Nikola Firentinac over the portal, possesses the town's most valuable paintings, by Francesco da Santacroce, Leandro Bassano and Palma the Younger. A 450-year-old cypress tree

stands in the cloister garden; in the refectory you can see the monumental 'Last Supper' (Venetian school, about 1600), as well as documents, manuscripts and a collection of Roman coins.

Links to Hvar via the car ferries: Split–Vita (1–3 times a day); Split–Stari Grad (1–3 times a day); Drvenik–Sećuraj (up to 11 times a day).

Shingle and rock beach, partly concreted. Many places suitable for bathing in the adjoining bays, on the *Devil's Islands* (especially *Palmižana* on *Sv. Clement*), and near the villages of *Milna*, *Sv. Nedjelija* and *Zavala* on the south coast of the island. Nude bathing on the island of *Jerolim* (10-minute boat trip), and on the other Paklenica (Devil's) Islands.

   S Hotel *Amfora*.

Hire of paddle boats and surfboards.

Hotels *Adriatic*, *Palace* (heated sea-water pool).

Heated sea-water pools of Olympic size in the Hotels *Amfora*, *Adriatic*, *Palace*, *Sirena*.

Course with free admission at the public 'Marble Baths'.

Near Milna and Palmižana (island of Sv. Clement).

Hotels *Amfora*, *Adriatic*, *Palace*.

Big leisure centre on the Fortica fortress, with speciality restaurants, wine bar and large terrace for dancing.

Summer festivals from the middle of June to the end of July, with theatrical and concert performances in the Arsenal, in the courtyard of San Marco, and on the open-air stage.

Korčula — a central-southern Dalmatian island

Regular performances on the open-air stage from the middle of July until September.

A pleasant walk around the bay (about 2 km, no motor traffic!), to the *Fortica* fortress (109 m, can be climbed comfortably in ½ hour); to the *Fortress of Napoleon,* from where there is a wonderful view of the western part of the island (241 m, ascent from the Stari Grad road).

To the *island of Biševo.* The island has a lot of caves and a Blue Grotto which according to experts vies with that on Capri.

Stari Grad Pop. 1700

You get the most beautiful view of Stari Grad if you come from Hvar by coach or car. About half-way you look down on the bay, which reaches inland for 6 km. On the narrow slopes lies the oldest settlement on the island of Hvar. You can easily understand why Stari Grad played a central role in marine trade for a long time, before being surpassed by Hvar. Sights include the remains of Illyrian *cyclopean walls,* an early Christian *baptistry* near the 12th c. church of *Sv. Ivan,* the Baroque *parish church* and the *Dominican monastery* which contains the 'Lamentation of Christ' by Tintoretto as well as a collection of coins and fossils. The main attraction of Stari Grad is the fortified *Tvrdalj summer residence* of the poet Petar Hektorović (1487–1572). Preserved in their original state are the entrance hall and the fish-pond, romantically encircled by arcades. Hektorović built the palace for himself and his friends — truly a place to inspire fine conversation.

Bathing on both sides of the long bay, part shingle, part rocks.

Jelsa

  Hotels *Adriatic* and *Arkada*.

 Dancing in the Hotels *Adriatic*, *Arkada* and *Helios*.

 Walks along the bay; along the road to *Vrbanj* (5 km) with remains of ancient fortifications, and from there a climb up the *Hum* (603 m).

Vrboska Pop. 500

Vrboska lies on a long, narrow bay, the south bank of which merges almost imperceptibly into the beaches of Jelsa. Vrboska is picturesque and enchanting, a little Venice with its bridges and two important churches: the original Renaissance fortified *Church of St Maria*, from the roof of which there is a lovely view, and the *Parish Church of St Laurentius* (built about 1500 and converted to the Baroque style) containing a noteworthy picture gallery which is remarkable for this little village (works by Veronese, Leandro Bassano and other masters of the Venetian school).

 The very beautiful *Soline* shingle beach, surrounded by pine trees, about 1 km from the village; naturist bathing on the island of *Zečevo*.

  Hotel *Adriatic*.

 Hire of rowing, motor and paddle boats, surfing centre (June 1st–October 15th).

Jelsa Pop. 1700

A quiet little town and harbour on the north coast of the island. It was mentioned in the 14th c. as a fishing settlement and the harbour for Pitve, which is situated higher up. The *parish church* was converted to its present form with the fortified apse in the 16th c., and the *main square*, with the little Baroque *Church of Sv. Ivan* and old houses, reminds you of olden days. In *Gradina*, to the east of the town, are to be found the Baroque *monastery church* of the Augustinians and the ruins of an older *defensive wall* (11th–12th c.).

A long shingle beach, with the beautiful bays of *Glavice* and *Grebisca;* naturist bathing on the island of Zečevo.

Sandolinos, rowing boats and motor boats can be hired at the harbour or through tourist agencies.

Boccia, basket-ball and hand-ball at the Hotel *Mina*.

Sand courts at the Hotel *Mina*.

Hotel *Mina*.

Hotels *Mina* and *Fontana*.

Hotels *Jadran* and *Mina*.

Pitve, *Park* restaurant, terrace for dancing in the Hotels *Genex*, *Fontana* and *Mina*.

Along the bay, to the *Augustinian monastery* (15 mins.). To *Humac*, an old village with picturesque houses, and to the neighbouring *Grotto of Grapčeva Špilia*, dating from the Neolithic period (10 km to the east). To *Zavala*, a little village with a beautiful beach on the south coast (about 6 km; the road leads through a 1400-m-long tunnel).

Dubrovnik

South Dalmatia and the Krka National Park

Dubrovnik Pop. 70,000

No description of Dubrovnik is possible without the use of superlatives. 'The Pearl of the Adriatic' even persuaded the waspish George Bernard Shaw to display an uncharacteristic outburst of feeling. He said that anyone seeking paradise on earth should go to Dubrovnik. From numerous places along the coast the local travel agents and couriers arrange excursions to Dubrovnik — mainly by coach, but also by hydrofoil. Visitors arriving by car should park well before they reach the

old town, which is barred to motor vehicles. As there are often cruise ships and car-ferries at anchor in the inner harbour basin, it can be difficult to drive through this area because of the vehicles waiting to embark.

 The history of Ragusa

Ragusa — the city was not officially named Dubrovnik until 1918 — was probably founded in the 7th c. by refugees from the Graeco-Roman settlement of Epidaurus (now Cavtat) on

View over the roof-tops of Old Dubrovnik

the island of Lave. The island was later joined to the mainland by the damming of the muddy channel, which today is the Placa Boulevard and main street. From the beginning, Ragusa was under Byzantine rule. At the end of the 12th c. the city elected its first prince and an aristocratic republic grew up, with great and lesser councils and a senate. At the head of the community stood the rector, whose residence was the rector's palace. In accordance with a very wise decision he was not allowed to hold office for longer than one month. From 1272 the city possessed its own statutes, based on administrative principles which appear modern even today. At the same time, by means of a number of trade agreements and political treaties, Dubrovnik safeguarded itself against potential enemies, laid claim to the Pelješac peninsula and Ston, the Konavle valley and the town of Cavtat, and thereby laid the foundations for its development into a powerful maritime republic and an independent miniature city state.

During the time of the Crusades (1205 to 1358) the city was under Venetian patronage, after the Peace of Zadar it belonged to the Hungarian-Croatian Empire, and it obtained complete independence in 1358. By means of tough diplomacy Dubrovnik retained its *de facto* independence for centuries, despite having recognised Turkish supremacy in the year 1458, and in spite of an attempt by Venice to get its hands on the city when it was struck by a serious earthquake in 1667. During its heyday in the 15th and 16th c., the little state was the strongest economic power on the east coast of the Adriatic; it traded with east and west, and enjoyed diplomatic relations with numerous states and cities. In 1806 Dubrovnik was occupied by French troops; in 1808 Marshal Marmont decreed that the republic should be dissolved. In the following year the city area was incorporated into Napoleon's 'Illyrian Provinces', and from 1815 to 1918 Dubrovnik, like the other coastal towns, belonged to Austria.

The encircling wall

Dubrovnik is said to be the most popular holiday resort on the Yugoslavian Adriatic coast. It is, without doubt, the chief tourist centre of the south. This comes as no surprise in view of its superb position in the midst of lush, subtropical vegetation, and its climate of sparse rainfall and abundant sunshine. A mighty encircling wall surrounds this beautiful city; this was started at the beginning of the 13th c. and was extended and strengthened until the end of the 17th c. by many master builders, including such famous ones as Juraj Dalmatinac.

This immense and solid bulwark around the old town has walls which are up to 25 m high, 4–6 m thick on the side facing the sea and 1½–3 m on the landward side. The structure is reinforced by three round and twelve square defensive towers, five bastions and two corner fortifications. It is barely 2 km around the inside, and if you enjoy walking this is a tour you should cer-tainly make. You will be rewarded with constantly changing views over the city, of the sea and the island of Lokrum, and of the hinterland with its range of karst mountains. There is a cableway to the top of the 412-m-high Brdo Srdj, from where there is a magnificent view. The walls, which are preserved in their original condition, can be entered under the bell-lodge in the east and near the church of Sveti Spas in the west.

📷 A walk round the city

Poljana Miličeva. Start your tour of the city at the western *Pile Gate* (16th c.). Steps lead down to the square called *Poljana Miličeva*. On the right is the great *Onofrio Fountain* (built in 1436 by Onofrio della Cava), a domed basin of sixteen sides, one of the termini of the old water-supply network. Behind it stands the former 13th c. Romanesque *Monastery of Sv. Clara* which now houses the Jadran restaurant and a conference and exhibition centre.

On the opposite side of the square

Part of the encircling wall, Dubrovnik

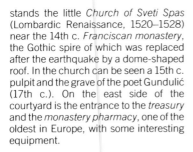

Overlooking the Placa

Sponza Palace

stands the little *Church of Sveti Spas* (Lombardic Renaissance, 1520–1528) near the 14th c. *Franciscan monastery*, the Gothic spire of which was replaced after the earthquake by a dome-shaped roof. In the church can be seen a 15th c. pulpit and the grave of the poet Gundulić (17th c.). On the east side of the courtyard is the entrance to the *treasury* and the *monastery pharmacy*, one of the oldest in Europe, with some interesting equipment.

Placa and Luža. Via the Placa or *Stradun,* the splendid main street of Dubrovnik with its 300-year-old flagstones, you come to the main square, the Luža, which has been the centre of public life of the city since earliest times.

Roland's Column (1418), the symbol of the medieval city of free trade, once also had a very practical function: a cubit, the official unit of length of the Republic of Dubrovnik, is chiselled into the right underarm of the warrior.

Sponza Palace. To the north lies the 16th c. Palais Sponza, formerly a customs-house, mint, treasury and bank; today there is a museum of the Socialist Revolution on the ground floor, with the archives of the Dubrovnik Republic housed on the upper floors. The palace has a beautiful Renaissance vestibule and arcaded courtyard.

Opposite the Sponza (also called Dogana or Divona) stands the Baroque *Church of St Blaise*, built over the old church of the city's patron saint which was burnt down in 1706. There is a silver statue of St Blaise, dating from the 14th/15th c., on the high altar. Completing the square are the *bell-lodge*, built in 1463, pulled down in the middle of the 19th c. and rebuilt in 1952, the *bell-tower* (15th c., completely restored in 1929) and the 18th c. *main police station*. In front of the police station is the *Little Onofrio Fountain* (mid 15th c.).

The Arsenal and Rector's Palace. Near the police station stand the *City Hall* and the 19th c. *National Theatre*. At one time the Municipal Council building and the Arsenal, which was demolished in the middle of the 19th c., with just a part still preserved in the harbour area, stood here. Adjoining the City Hall is the Rector's Palace, built by Onofrio della Cava between 1435 and 1441, in place of the old castle-like palace which had been destroyed by a gunpowder explosion. The Florentine Renaissance master-builder Michelozzo was involved in the restoration — he built the Renaissance portico — and the completion of the palace is attributed to Juraj Dalmatinac. In the Rector's Palace are housed a museum of cultural history and the library of the Dubrovnik Theological College, with incunabula and documents from the 15th to the 18th c.

Cathedral of the Virgin Mary. Diagonally opposite stands the Baroque Cathedral of the Virgin Mary, built in the 17th c. in place of the old Romanesque cathedral

St Blaise

which had been destroyed by an earthquake. Richard the Lionheart is said to have endowed the church as a thanksgiving for his deliverance after being shipwrecked near the island of Lokrum when returning from the Third Crusade. The cathedral houses a wealth

The Golden Age of Dubrovnik displayed in the Rector's Palace

The harbour, Dubrovnik

of treasures. Among the numerous paintings by Italian and native masters is the winged-altar representation of the 'Assumption of the Virgin Mary' (Titian school) above the high altar. The treasury is one of the richest in Yugoslavia and is open two mornings a week. Worthy of special note is the collection of reliquaries, comprising 138 items.

Altar in the Cathedral of the Virgin Mary

Jesuit Church of St Ignatius. Going westwards from the cathedral, you pass the Jesuit Church, built between 1699 and 1725. The church tower contains the oldest bell in Dubrovnik, dating from 1355. You then proceed along Strossmayer Street to the *Rupe* (16th c., restored 1940), which was previously a grain store with fifteen subterranean cisterns hewn out of the rock; today it is a municipal museum.

Dominican Monastery. Of the more than thirty former churches in the city, special mention should be made of the *Orthodox Church*, because of its rich collection of icons in the parish office situated in Ulica od Puča, the main business street, and also of the Dominican Monastery (14th/15th c.),

Right: View over Dubrovnik

Main street, Dubrovnik

north-east of the Sponza. Especially noteworthy are its wonderful cloisters and in the church a painting by Titian, 'Mary Magdalene'. Here and in the monastery you will find a remarkable collection of other paintings, including some by the Dubrovnik school.

Mostar Pop. 90,000
The Turkish bridge over the Neretva at

Restaurant overlooking Dubrovnik

Mostar is known to almost everybody, appearing as it does on so many brochures and advertisements. It was built in 1566, during the Ottoman occupation of a large part of the Balkans, which lasted almost 400 years. It was during this period that the oriental character of the old town was shaped, by the building of slender minarets, mosques and some Turkish dwelling houses now used as museums, which can be visited.

The bridge elegantly spans the river by means of a single arch. When it was built there had already been a settlement on the river for at least 100 years. However, the town's present name derives from the word *Mostari*, meaning 'keepers of the bridge'.

Mostar lies in a broad basin. There are vineyards all round the town, as far as

Leading to Dubrovnik harbour

Turkish Bridge, Mostar

Domed burial vault, Mostar

At Mostar

the eye can see; the grapes are ripened in the constant summer heat. From this district come the two kinds of wine which can be bought everywhere, white Zilavka and red Plavac.

Visiting Mostar in summer is an exhausting pleasure, especially since the coaches from the coastal resorts never arrive until about midday, when the heat is at its greatest.

The old part of the town lies mainly on the left bank of the Neretva. The way on foot to the bridge leads past the *Karadoz Beg Mosque,* built in 1557 and the largest of the fourteen mosques in the town. It is particularly impressive because of its tall and slender minaret. Then you come to the *Koski Mehmet Mosque,* in front of which stands a Turkish domed burial vault with a sarcophagus. Just before you reach the bridge is the *Kujundziluk,* a row of cafés and shops selling souvenirs, filigree work and jewellery.

On your journey to Mostar from the coast, you should spare time for three further visits: to the oriental-looking *Počitelj* with a castle above the Neretva, to the *Bogumil tombs* with Glagolitic inscriptions, near Stolac and Radimlje, and to the *Buna Spring,* in which a river rises directly from a natural arch in the rock.

🚌 Pilgrimage to Medjugorje

Medjugorje, in the karst mountain area of Hercegovina, is only 30 km from Mostar. There are daily excursions to this place of pilgrimage from the Dalmatian coast. It is said that since June 24th 1981 children have been receiving messages from the Virgin Mary, which are passed on to the pilgrims. Believers come by charter-plane from all parts of the world, via the airports at Split, Dubrovnik and Zadar. Local and foreign coach companies organise visits lasting several days. Private guest-houses, hotels and bungalow complexes provide accommodation all the year round for many thousands of visitors.

In order to cope with the demand, Medjugorje will no doubt be developing for some time to come.

Trsteno

A visit to the *Villa Gozze Park* is a memorable experience. The park was laid out in 1502 in Trsteno, 30 km from Dubrovnik. Two giant plane trees, with trunks of more than 10 m in circumference, can be seen from the coast road which runs past the park. Nearby is the entrance to a unique collection of exotic trees and plants.

The Krka National Park

The River Krka rises a few kilometres east of Knin (see page 36), winds through steep gorges, fans out into wide, peaceful lakes and, in the 60 km of its course, forms no less than eight cataracts. For those who have the time and inclination to spend a few days of their holiday in an unusual way, here is a brief description.

The first waterfall of the river, the only one along its upper course, is near the source. Seven kilometres downstream from Knin the river widens to become the *Marasović Lake,* and then plunges over rocky banks 16 m high near *Bilušci* to form its second waterfall. This is where the middle reach begins. After spreading out into *Lake Bijelob*, the river divides into several arms which, in as many cascades, form the third waterfall of *Ćorić*. This is immediately followed by

the fourth, generally acknowledged to be the finest — three mighty terraces 62 m high make up the *Manojlovac Falls. Sondovjel* is less impressive and lies amid a lonely, barren landscape. The area then becomes fertile and more attractive near the falls of *Milječka,* followed later by towering walls of rugged and fissured rock, with the ruins of the *castles* of *Trošenj* and *Nečvem* to the right and left of the river. Twelve kilometres before reaching the mighty *Roškislap Falls* it is worth paying a visit to the *Sv. Arkandel Monastery of the Archangels*, with its interesting treasury.

On a small island in a lake-like stretch of the river behind Babingrad, surrounded by steep walls of rock, stands the romantic *Franciscan Friary* of *Visovac*. The island was originally occupied by Augustinian monks, until Franciscans arrived from Bosnia in

Franciscan Friary at Visovac

Krka waterfalls

1445. Having fought strenuously against the Turks in the 16th c., the friars took fright and fled to Šibenik. In 1674, however, the Turkish Sultan Mehmed IV magnanimously allowed them to return. The tranquil *cloisters*, the *church* and especially the *library*, with an early Croatian edition of Aesop's fables and 620 documents and manuscripts from the troubled Turkish period, form the main attraction for visitors.

The Krka Waterfalls

Seven kilometres south of Visovac you come to the *Skradinski buk,* the eighth, last and biggest cataract of all which, depending on the water-level, cascades from a height of 45 m, in 17 steps, over five terraces some 100 m wide. It is very pleasant to sit under the shady trees, facing the sparkling, spraying waters, and enjoy freshly caught and crisply fried Krka trout.

The 14,000 or so hectares around the Krka waterfalls have been a protected area since 1968. In view of the 400,000 visitors who come to see this natural spectacle every year, it was found necessary in 1988 to impose further restrictions and to declare it a national park. Thus, for instance, there is now a ban on swimming in the basins between the terraces of the waterfalls, in order to protect the mosses and chalk-deposits.

To reach Krka National Park you can travel by boat from Šibenik to Skradin. Car drivers will find the route signposted from the Adria-Magistrale to the national park. In Trumilija the road forks: the left fork leads to Skradin, the right one to the entrance to the park, which is open between 8 a.m. and 8 p.m. During the high season all vehicles have to be left on the upper car park. You pay your entrance-fee at the gate and take a shuttle-bus to the river deep down in the valley. Out of season it is possible to drive to the small lower car park.

You can also leave the car on a large car park in Skradin, walk to the landing-stage on the quay and take one of the boats, which leave hourly between 9.30 a.m. and 3.30 p.m., for the first and largest of the waterfalls.

From the lower car park near the main entrance to the national park, there is a choice of two boat trips: a one-hour trip, which starts at the upper edge of the waterfall and goes round the banks of the lakes, and a four-hour trip with a visit to the monastery island.

Skradin

Useful things to know

Before you go

Climate and when to go

Dalmatia has a Mediterranean-type climate with hot dry summers and mild wet winters. The main holiday season is from April to October. In July and August the seaside resorts and camping sites are very crowded and for those who prefer a quieter holiday, it is best, if possible, to choose April and May, or September and October. Many hotels stay open throughout the year. (For further details see Holidays in Dalmatia, page 7.)

Accommodation

Yugoslavian hotels in the large resorts and holiday areas on the coast are up to international standard. Most visitors book package tours, but if travelling independently it is essential to reserve hotel accommodation in advance, especially in the popular resorts.

Camping and caravanning: Many of the sites are very well equipped but as camping is very popular in Yugoslavia they become very crowded in the summer. Off-site camping is not encouraged although local authorities will sometimes help visitors who wish to camp on private land where there is no official site. A list of camp sites is available from the Yugoslavian National Tourist Office (see page 95).

Youth hostels: For young people these offer reasonably priced accommodation. During the holiday season it is advisable to book in advance. Visitors must be members of the national Youth Hostels Association of their own country.

Insurance

If you are taking a package holiday, this will almost certainly include the option of full holiday insurance with a reputable company. If you are making your own travel arrangements, you are strongly recommended to take out a suitable policy. Normal cover will provide protection against such misfortunes as cancellation or curtailment, medical and associated expenses (this is particularly important), baggage and personal effects, money, personal accident and personal liability.

If you are taking a car, you must inform your insurance company in good time, and obtain a 'Green Card' to provide you with cover in those countries through which you will pass, as well as in Yugoslavia itself.

What to take

Yugoslavia is well organised for tourism and you will be able to buy most of what you need there, including the essential suntan lotion and films for your camera.

You will not need to take any formal clothes but many hotels expect their guests to be suitably dressed for dinner and request that bikinis or beach wear are not worn in the public rooms. As Yugoslavia has few sandy beaches, it is advisable to wear bathing-shoes on the shingle and rocky beaches, as you can expect to come across sea-urchins.

First-aid kit. It is advisable to take a simple first-aid kit with you. This should include any medicines which have been prescribed for you or which you regularly use at home plus remedies for stomach and digestive upsets, headaches and colds, and a supply of pain-killers.

For minor injuries pack an elastic bandage, plasters, an antiseptic and anti-inflammatory cream. If your eyes are sensitive to light or strain take some eye-drops or ointment.

Getting to Yugoslavia

By air: Most visitors to Yugoslavia from Great Britain travel by air, the majority on package holidays. These generally use charter flights to the coastal airports of Pula, Dubrovnik, Zadar and Split. There are also scheduled services between major British airports and Pula, Dubrovnik and Split.

By rail: The following coastal towns can be reached by rail — Rijeka, Zadar, Šibenik, Split, Kardeljevo and Bar; from these places the other coastal towns can be reached quickly by coach. From London to Split by train takes about 40 hours.

By road: It is a very long drive from Great Britain to Yugoslavia. There are, however, overnight motorail services from Stuttgart and Munich to Rijeka and from Brussels to Ljubljana from June until September. During the summer the traffic is very heavy on the 1035-km-long Adria-Magistrale; because of the many bends it is sometimes dangerous to overtake lorries, which often travel slowly. Instead of crossing the border at Trieste and then having to drive down the whole length of the coast to reach the Dalmatian resorts, you can take alternative routes through the interior.

By sea: Car ferries operate between Italy and the Dalmatian coast: Ancona–Zadar, Ancona–Split, Venice–Zadar and Bari–Dubrovnik.

Immigration and Customs

Passports: You are advised to allow at least eight weeks to obtain or renew a full British passport. Alternatively, a British Visitor's Passport, which can be obtained from most main post offices, is valid for entry into Yugoslavia.

Vehicle documents: A visitor bringing a private car into Yugoslavia must have in his possession a driving licence and registration document. The border officials are sure to ask to see your Green Card (for caravans as well). If you cannot produce one you will have to take out a short-period Yugoslavian motor insurance policy.

Entry: The following are free from customs duty when you enter Yugoslavia (per person over the age of 16 years): 200 cigarettes or 50 cigars or 250 grammes of tobacco, 1 litre of wine and ¾ litre of spirits, 1 kg of coffee and ¼ litre of toilet water. All items must be declared. You will have no difficulty in taking personal effects through in quantities which do not have any commercial implications: two cameras, a film or video camera, a pair of binoculars, a portable radio or television, a portable typewriter, camping, sports and fishing equipment.

Foreign currency in any form (cash, travellers' cheques, Giro cheques, personal cheques etc.) can be taken into Yugoslavia.

Exit: Yugoslavian money may be exported only up to certain limits, the amount of which can be ascertained from the Yugoslavian tourist offices. Gifts may be taken out of the country (or posted abroad) in unlimited quantities, as long as it can be proved that they were purchased with foreign currency which the holidaymaker brought into the country. Objects of archaeological, historical or particular artistic value may be exported only with a special licence issued by the *Central Office for the Protection of Historical Monuments*.

During your stay
Currency

The unit of currency in Yugoslavia is the dinar. Inflation is rampant; this is vividly illustrated by the fact that in December 1988 the rate of exchange was approximately 10,000 dinars to the pound sterling and by August 1989 this had become 29,700! (subject to limit). Inflation has led to the printing of banknotes for ever-increasing values; in 1988 50,000-dinar notes were introduced which are now worth about £1.68. It is advisable to exchange sterling for dinars only in the country itself and, as the rates of exchange alter every day, only in small amounts.

When changing money it is advisable to keep receipts, which are necessary if dinars are subsequently changed back into sterling.

Yugoslavian money may be exported only up to certain limits; the amount can be ascertained from tourist offices. (Note: although sterling can be exchanged into dinars on international trains at frontier stations on entry, there are no similar facilities when leaving the country by rail.)

Electricity

This is generally at 220 volts A.C.; it is advisable to take a Continental adaptor (available from any electrical supplier).

Fishing

Sea-fishing is allowed in principle, except in harbours, public bathing places and special zones (reserves). Anyone fishing from a boat needs a licence. Fishing in streams, rivers or lakes is permitted only with the agreement of the local authority, the *'Opština Skupština'*.

Newspapers

During the season, many British newspapers and periodicals can be obtained without difficulty in all the larger towns. However, as they have to be flown in by airmail they are somewhat dearer than in the U.K.

Opening times

Banks are generally open 8 a.m.– noon and 4.30–7 p.m. on Mondays to Fridays, and 8 a.m.–noon on Saturdays. In the larger holiday resorts these hours are sometimes extended and you should make enquiries locally.

Government offices are usually open 7 a.m.–3 p.m.

Shops are open 8 a.m.–noon and 5–8 p.m. on Mondays to Saturdays. Larger stores stay open from 8 a.m. to 8 p.m. (3 p.m. on Saturdays).

Post and telephone

Postage stamps can be obtained at post offices and postcard stands and from hotel reception desks.

Since inflation has put most coins out of circulation, you can normally make calls only via the operator at the post office (PTT). You wait to be shown to a cubicle, and then dial the number yourself. In some smaller post offices the clerk will dial the country code for you. You will always be given a slip showing the amount to pay. In some towns magnetic phone-cards can be used, but you should always be prepared for a longish wait. To phone the U.K. from Yugoslavia, first dial 9944 followed by the local S.T.D. code (minus the first '0') and then the subscriber's number. To ring Yugoslavia from abroad the number is 010 38, followed by the town code and the subscriber's number.

Public Holidays

There are public holidays on January 1st, May 1st and November 1st. On May 27th Slovenia celebrates the founding of the Liberation Front of the Slovenian People, and on July 22nd the Day of the Slovene People's Uprising. There are also national holidays on July 4th (Day of the Freedom Fighters) and on November 29th (Day of the Founding of the Republic). New Year, Labour Day and the National Holiday celebrations last two days; if one of these is a Sunday then an extra day is added.

Time

Yugoslavia observes Central European Time, i.e. one hour ahead of G.M.T., with clocks put forward one hour during the summer.

Tipping

Tips are, of course, expected and — like everywhere else in the world — they make life easier. Do not assume that tips are included in the cost of a package holiday; what is included is the service charge, and if you get particularly good service from a waiter, room-maid, taxi- or coach-driver, you should recognise it by means of a tip. Moreover, the staff are often employed only during the holiday season, and it may well be that a whole family has to exist for a year on the income from those four or six months. Quite apart from that, it is not the size of the tip, but the recognition of a difficult job well done which is being acknowledged.

Traffic regulations

Speed limits are 60 km p.h. in towns, 80 or sometimes 100 km p.h. on normal roads and 120 km p.h. on motorways. Trams generally have priority. The traffic police are particularly active on the motorways. Fines have to be paid on the spot. Accidents resulting in damage or bodily injury must be reported to the police. The emergency numbers anywhere in the country are: police 92, rescue service 94, breakdowns 987.

Petrol: Usually available in 95 and 98 octane. An increasing number of petrol stations on the coast and along the most important through-routes now sell lead-free petrol.

Safety on the road: The Adria-Magistrale is particularly dangerous if it rains after a long period of drought, when a greasy film of oil, water and dust is formed. The coastal section of the Magistrale has had many bends roughened with grooves to prevent skidding. However, this road remains a risk, especially when rain and the *Bora* wind occur at the same time. This gusty north wind can blow lorries, coaches and even caravans off the road. Car-drivers also have to adjust to the fact that most of the tunnels in the country are not lit.

Transport in the area

Buses: The Dalmatian coast has a good network of local bus services.

Car hire: Several international car-hire firms now have branches in the country (Hertz, Avis, Inter-Rent etc.). There are also the Yugoslavian hire firms of Inex, Putnik and Unis. In the busy season, however, you should reserve well in advance through your travel agent. There are no local car-hire firms. Yugoslavian travel agents will also arrange cars for you, as will the couriers in the holiday areas. There are no hotel garages in Yugoslavia and only a few manned car-parks.

Ferries: Numerous ferries, many transporting cars, link harbours on the mainland with the principal offshore islands.

Underwater sport

Diving with oxygen cylinders and the taking of underwater photographs are allowed only in some areas of the Adriatic coast. The local tourist bureaux will provide information.

Archaeological exploration under-water requires, in addition, a permit from the relevant authority concerned with the protection of ancient monuments. Information can be obtained from: Zavod za sportski ribolov na moru i podvodne aktivnosti SFRJ, Rijeka, Matije Gupca 2.

Important addresses

British Embassy,
General Ždanova 46,
11000 Belgrade; tel. 64 50 55, 64 50 43, 64 50 34 and 64 50 87.

There are British Consular Offices at Belgrade, Zagreb and Split.

Yugoslav Embassy,
5–7 Lexham Gardens,
London W8 5JJ; tel. (01) 370 6105.

Yugoslav Tourist Office,
143 Regent Street,
London W1R 8AE; tel. (01) 734 5243, (01) 743 8714 and (01) 439 0399.

Index